ANDREW DIOSY

YOU HAVE TO SEE THIS

LINDA LEE

MASTER POINT PRESS

Master Point Press
22 Lower Village Gate
Toronto, Ontario, Canada
M5P 3L7
(416) 932-9766
Internet www.pathcom.com/~raylee/

Distributed in the U.S.A. by Barricade Books
150 Fifth Avenue, Suite 700
New York, NY 10011
(800) 59-BOOKS

Canadian Cataloguing in Publication Data

Diosy, Andrew, 1924-
  You have to see this

ISBN 0-9698461-9-3

1. Contract bridge — Defensive play. 2. Contract bridge — Dummy play.
I. Lee, Linda (Linda Marcia), 1947-. II. Title.

GV1282.43.D56 1998   795.41'53   C98-930835-9

Cover and book design	Olena Serbyn
Additional Analysis	Bill Milgram
	Colin Lee

Printed and bound in Canada

1 2 3 4 5 6 7   04 03 02 01 00 99 98

Table of Contents

Table of Contents

Introduction

Readers of Andrew Diosy's first book *There Must Be A Way* will be tempted to skip this section and get right into the hands, but they shouldn't. There are several differences between that volume and the present one. New readers will find the format a little unusual. Unlike the usual run of books of bridge problems, this one, like the first, rarely tells you whether you are declarer trying to make a hand, or a defender trying to come up with the right play to beat it. Instead, you are generally given all four hands, the contract, the bidding where relevant, and the opening lead. Your task is to determine the result, given best play and defence. Imagine you are relaxing with friends after a bridge session; was there some way you could have made that slam? Would a switch at trick 2 have beaten them on the last hand? You get the idea.

The format of the solutions is a little different here, too. Many of these hands are such that the obvious 'solution' fails, given best play by both sides; one or the other has some subtle counter-move. All the hands appear on a right-hand page, and overleaf is the first part of the solution. This will give you some hint as to the direction you should be looking, and may well explain why your first ideas don't quite work. The 'final' solutions are gathered together in a separate section at the back of the book. Bidding on 52-card layouts is given only where it is helpful or indicative of a useful approach to the real-life problem. The single dummy hands can all be made via a reasonably logical line of play.

Level of difficulty is subjective; not everyone will agree with our division of the hands into 'Not Too Hard', 'Pretty Difficult', and 'Really Challenging'. But we'll warn you that some of them will test your powers of analysis to the limit, however good you are! Eddie Kantar, in his foreword to *There Must Be A Way*, warned readers not to try to solve too many at one sitting and we must echo that here, too. Savour them as you would haute cuisine in a fine restaurant, rather than 'All You Can Eat' fast food. In the process, you'll come across neat plays and stratagems that you can begin to look for at the table.

Most of these hands came up in actual play, and surprisingly often the declarer or defenders managed to do the right thing under fire. How will you do?

Andrew Diosy
Linda Lee
Toronto, September 1998

SECTION 1

NOT TOO HARD

HAND 1 • *Extra Chance*

NORTH
♠ K
♡ A K 10 3
◇ A Q 10 9
♣ K Q 10 2

WEST
♠ Q J 10 5
♡ 8 7
◇ J 5 2
♣ A 7 6 4

EAST
♠ 9 7 6 4 3 2
♡ Q 9 5
◇ 4
♣ J 9 8

SOUTH
♠ A 8
♡ J 6 4 2
◇ K 8 7 6 3
♣ 5 3

Contract: 6◇

Opening Lead: ♠Q

HAND 2 • *On Your Toes*

NORTH
♠ 5 3
♡ A 10 4
◇ Q 8 7 6
♣ K 10 3 2

WEST
♠ K 8 6 4
♡ 7
◇ 10 5 4 2
♣ 9 8 5 4

EAST
♠ A Q 10 9 7
♡ K 5 2
◇ K J 9 3
♣ J

SOUTH
♠ J 2
♡ Q J 9 8 6 3
◇ A
♣ A Q 7 6

W	N	E	S
		1♠	2♡
pass	3♡	pass	4♡
all pass			

Contract: 4♡

Opening Lead: ♠4

HAND 1 • *Extra Chance*

Playing rubber bridge, you are rather pleased to arrive at this excellent slam. Since the loss of a club trick seems unavoidable, success seems to depend on the heart finesse. As we can see, the heart queen is guarded and offside.

Obviously, if declarer could establish two winners in the club suit for two heart discards from hand, the heart loser could be avoided and the slam made. On winning the ♠K, declarer draws three rounds of trumps and leads up to the club suit in dummy. However, when West ducks the ♣A, there is no way to return to the hand to lead another club towards the ♣Q. But if clubs are led from dummy, there appears to be no way to establish two more club tricks for discards.

Is there any way to find some extra chance which will allow declarer to make this slam? See page 68 for the second part of the answer.

HAND 2 • *On Your Toes*

After the opening spade lead, East wins the ♠A and leads the ♣J angling for a club ruff. Hoping to avoid the club ruff declarer leads a trump to the ♡A and continues with a second heart, East winning. Now East leads a small spade to West's ♠K and gets his heart ruff. The defence is on its toes. Well done. But wait — is there any way that declarer can head off defeat? See page 68 for the second part of the answer.

HAND 3 • *Safety Play*

NORTH
♠ J 10 6 2
♡ A Q
◇ K J 5
♣ 9 6 4 3

Opening Lead: ◇ 10
Contract: 6♠

SOUTH
♠ A K 9 8 5 4
♡ 7
◇ A 4
♣ A K J 2

South wins the first trick, and cashes the ♠A. West shows out, but declarer can still make the hand regardless of the distribution of the rest of the suits.

HAND 4 • *Routine*

NORTH
♠ A K 5 4
♡ 10 8 6 2
◇ Q 9 2
♣ 7 3

WEST
♠ 10 8 6 3 2
♡ J 9 5
◇ 8 5
♣ J 10 5

EAST
♠ J
♡ K 7 4 3
◇ A J 10 7 6
♣ A 9 8

SOUTH
♠ Q 9 7
♡ A Q
◇ K 4 3
♣ K Q 6 4 2

W	N	E	S
		1◇	1NT
pass	3NT	all pass	

Contract: 3 NT
Opening Lead: ◇ 8

HAND 3 • *Safety Play*

Answer Part 1

South has eleven winners off the top: six spades, two diamonds, one heart and two clubs. He therefore needs to find just one more winner in one of his side suits, and he can afford to give up one trick to set this up. Clubs seems like the most likely source of his twelfth trick but there are also possible extra tricks in both of the red suits. Perhaps there is an endplay that would guarantee a twelfth trick or perhaps a safety play in the club suit.

Can you see the right line? See page 69 for the second part of the answer

HAND 4 • *Routine*

Answer Part 1

The opening diamond lead goes to the ◇9 and ◇10 and South wins with the ◇K. Declarer has three spades, a heart and a diamond off the top. It seems obvious to attack clubs, so declarer crosses to the dummy with the ♠A and leads a club to the king. He then crosses back on the second spade and leads another club. Whether East wins the ♣A or ducks it, South is home. He can establish clubs and in fact can make an overtrick if he chooses to finesse the ♡Q.

Is there any alternative line for the defence? Is this hand cold? See page 70 for the second part of the answer.

HAND 5 • *Elementary, My Dear Watson*

NORTH
♠ 6 4 3
♡ Q 8 7 5
♢ A Q 10 7
♣ Q 5

W	N	E	S
pass	pass	pass	1♡
pass	3♡	pass	4♡
all pass			

Opening Lead: ♣A

SOUTH
♠ A Q 2
♡ A K J 9 4 3 2
♢ 8
♣ 8 4

West starts off by cashing the top two clubs and switches to a trump won by the ♡A, East following.

HAND 6 • *When The Going Gets Tough, the Tough Take a Finesse*

NORTH
♠ J 6 5 2
♡ K
♢ K 6
♣ K Q 9 5 4 2

WEST
♠ A 8 7
♡ J 7
♢ 9 7 4 3
♣ A 10 8 3

EAST
♠ 10 3
♡ Q 10 4 2
♢ J 8 5 2
♣ J 7 6

SOUTH
♠ K Q 9 4
♡ A 9 8 6 5 3
♢ A Q 10
♣ —

Contract: 6♠
Opening Lead: ♠A

HAND 5 • *Elementary, My Dear Watson*

Answer Part 1

There are four potential losers on this hand, the two top clubs and two spade tricks. While it is true that East is likely to have the ♠K since West did not open the bidding and has already shown up with the ace and king of clubs, there may be extra chances even if the ♠K is offside. For example, you could finesse the ◇Q. If the finesse wins you are home, since you now have a discard for one of your spade losers. Even if the finesse loses, you can discard your small spade on the ◇A and fall back on the spade finesse. This was the line taken by declarer at one table. Sherlock Holmes was sitting at the other table and he found a better line. Can you? See page 70 for the second part of the answer.

HAND 6 • *When The Going Gets Tough, the Tough Take a Finesse*

Answer Part 1

Declarer is off the trump ace and can therefore not afford to lose another trick. One way to play the hand is to attempt to set up the heart suit. If the suit splits 3-3 this could be done easily with one ruff, but with a 4-2 split declarer is going to need two ruffs. This appears possible even though the defence has started with a trump lead, but entries are going to be a bit of a problem. Suppose West continues with a second trump: South wins in hand and cashes the ♡K, crossing back to his hand with a diamond. South ruffs a heart and cashes the ◇K, but cannot get back to his hand twice, first to ruff a heart and then to cash the suit.

Is there a way to create the critical hand entries? See page 72 for the second part of the answer.

HAND 7 • *About Finesses*

NORTH
♠ Q 10 8 6 2
♡ A Q 2
◊ K 7 3
♣ 7 2

WEST
♠ 7 5 4
♡ J
◊ J 8
♣ K J 9 8 5 4 3

EAST
♠ —
♡ K 9 8 7 5
◊ Q 10 6 5 4 2
♣ 10 6

SOUTH
♠ A K J 9 3
♡ 10 6 4 3
◊ A 9
♣ A Q

W	N	E	S
			1♠
3♣	4♠	pass	4NT
pass	5◊	pass	6♠
all pass			

Contract: 6♠

Opening Lead: ♡J

HAND 8 • *Numero Uno*

NORTH
♠ K 3
♡ 9 6 4
◊ J 5 3
♣ Q 8 6 4 2

North-South vul.

W	N	E	S
			1♡
3♠	pass	pass	dbl
pass	4♡	all pass	

Opening Lead: ◊A

SOUTH
♠ J 9
♡ A K Q 8 3
◊ K 6 4 2
♣ A K

East plays an encouraging ◊ 10 at trick one, but West switches to the ♣J. After drawing trumps (West has two) you cash the other top club and both follow. Can you make this hand?

HAND 7 • *About Finesses*

Answer Part 1

There are three potential losers: a club and two hearts. This is a hand where it is not right to take any finesses. Declarer wins the opening heart lead with the ♡A and draws trumps in three rounds. Now it is possible to eliminate diamonds and throw West in on a club. West will be endplayed and forced to give declarer a ruff-sluff. However, declarer is still left with an inevitable heart loser. Can declarer do better on best defence? See page 72 for the second part of the answer.

HAND 8 • *Numero Uno*

Answer Part 1

South has five potential losers: three diamonds and two spades. However, dummy has a source of tricks in the club suit if it can be reached. Unfortunately the ♠A is very likely to be in the East hand (assuming West would not pre-empt with two aces) so you will not be able to enter dummy that way. If you lead the ♠9 to the ♠10 and the ♠K, the defence will cash the other spade and lead a third spade, leaving you to play diamonds from your hand. If only you could endplay East...Bob Hamman is South at the other table and is sure to give the best play. Better take another look. See page 72 for the second part of the answer.

HAND 9 • *The Forcing Defence*

NORTH
♠ J 7 6 4
♡ A K 8 5 4 2
♢ —
♣ 8 6 2

WEST
♠ 3
♡ 10 3
♢ K 8 4 3 2
♣ A K Q 10 5

EAST
♠ K 8 5 2
♡ Q 9
♢ Q J 7 6 5
♣ 9 7

SOUTH
♠ A Q 10 9
♡ J 7 6
♢ A 10 9
♣ J 4 3

W	N	E	S
			1♠
2NT	4♠	dbl	all pass

Contract: 4♠ doubled
Opening Lead: ♣A

HAND 10 • *Trump Promotion*

NORTH
♠ —
♡ 3
♢ Q 8 7 6 5 4 3
♣ K Q J 3 2

WEST
♠ 10 4 3 2
♡ A 9 8 7
♢ A 10
♣ 9 8 7

EAST
♠ 9 8 7 6 5
♡ 4
♢ K J 9
♣ A 10 6 4

SOUTH
♠ A K Q J
♡ K Q J 10 6 5 2
♢ 2
♣ 5

Contract: 4♡
Opening Lead: ♢A

HAND 9 • *The Forcing Defence*

Answer Part 1

This hand occurred several years ago at a European championship. West starts with three rounds of clubs. Now what? If West now switches to a heart, declarer wins, finesses the spade, re-enters dummy with a diamond ruff and continues with the ♠J. Despite the bad spade break, declarer can make the hand since after drawing all the trumps, he finds that the heart suit breaks 2-2. Suppose West continues with a fourth club: does this change the situation? See page 73 for the second part of the answer.

HAND 10 • *Trump Promotion*

Answer Part 1

Against four hearts, the defence starts off with two rounds of diamonds, ruffed by declarer. There are only three top losers in this hand: a heart, a club and a diamond. The danger is that the defence can promote a second trump trick. Suppose declarer leads a high heart and West wins. He crosses to his partner's hand on the ♣A and East leads the third diamond. Now if South ruffs high, West's ♡9 will eventually set up and if he does not, West will score the setting trick right now.

Can you see any hope for declarer? Can the defence counter? See page 73 for the second part of the answer.

HAND 11 • *The Right Hand*

NORTH
♠ A 10 9 5 2
♡ A 4
◇ J 7 2
♣ Q 8 7

WEST
♠ 4
♡ K 9 8 7 3
◇ 6 5 4
♣ K 10 6 2

EAST
♠ K 8 6 3
♡ 10 6 5
◇ K 10 8 3
♣ A 5

SOUTH
♠ Q J 7
♡ Q J 2
◇ A Q 9
♣ J 9 4 3

Contract: 3NT
Opening Lead: ♡7

HAND 12 • *Know Your Odds*

NORTH
♠ A Q
♡ 6 5
◇ A K Q
♣ A J 7 5 4 3

WEST
♠ J 9 7 3
♡ Q 10 2
◇ 10 9
♣ K 10 9 2

EAST
♠ 10 8 5
♡ J 8 7 3
◇ 8 7 6 4 3
♣ 8

SOUTH
♠ K 6 4 2
♡ A K 9 4
◇ J 5 2
♣ Q 6

Contract: 6NT
Opening Lead: ♠3

HAND 11 • *The Right Hand*

Answer Part 1

After winning the opening heart lead with the ♡J, declarer plays the ♠Q, letting it run, and continues with the ♠J, West showing out. Declarer now has two heart tricks, four spade tricks (once he gives up the ♠K) and a diamond trick. He must find two more tricks. East ducks the second spade, wins the third round of spades with the ♠K and continues hearts, dummy's ♡A winning. Even though the diamond finesse works, declarer still falls a trick short.

Can you improve on this line? See page 74 for the second part of the answer.

HAND 12 • *Know Your Odds*

Answer Part 1

South counted three spade tricks, three diamond tricks and two heart tricks, so he needed four tricks from the club suit. Winning the ♠Q, declarer crossed to hand on the ♡A. Any 3-2 club division would make the hand easy, but what about a 4-1 split? Declarer might try cashing the ♣A, as a safety play in case of a singleton ♣K, but the odds are three times greater that the singleton is the ♣8, ♣9 or ♣10. The odds therefore favour running the ♣Q, which would be covered with the ♣K and ♣A. Now if South had no entry problems, he could cross to hand and lead the ♣6, covered with the ♣10 and ♣J, and concede a trick to West's ♣9 holding his club losers to one. But the only way for South to return to his hand is with the ♡K, and this opens up the heart suit for the defence.

Is there any way out of this conundrum? See page 74 for the second part of the answer.

HAND 13 • *A Failed Effort*

NORTH
♠ K Q 9
♡ 8 6 3
◇ Q 10 7 6 5
♣ Q J

WEST
♠ 10 8 7 3
♡ K Q 10
◇ K 4
♣ A 10 7 3

EAST
♠ 6 5 4
♡ J 9 7 2
◇ J 9 2
♣ 8 5 2

SOUTH
♠ A J 2
♡ A 5 4
◇ A 8 3
♣ K 9 6 4

W	N	E	S
1♣	pass	pass	dbl
pass	3◇	pass	3NT
all pass			

Contract: 3NT
Opening Lead: ♡K

HAND 14 • *Your Long Suit*

NORTH
♠ A J 9 7 5 2
♡ Q 4
◇ A 7
♣ A K 10

WEST
♠ K 6
♡ 8 7 5 2
◇ K J 3 2
♣ 9 8 3

EAST
♠ 10 8 4 3
♡ 9 6
◇ 9 8 5
♣ Q 6 5 2

SOUTH
♠ Q
♡ A K J 10 3
◇ Q 10 6 4
♣ J 7 4

Contract: 6♡
Opening Lead: ♣9

HAND 13 • *A Failed Effort*

Answer Part 1

West finds the fine lead of the ♡K. Declarer ducks two rounds and wins the third heart. Declarer has five top tricks, and the diamond suit offers the best hope of getting the remaining tricks. Declarer starts with the ◇A and continues with a diamond to West's ◇K. West is helpless and cannot reach the East hand for the long heart. The hand is cold — or is it? Can the defence do better — is there a way to get the East hand in? See page 74 for the second part of the answer.

HAND 14 • *Your Long Suit*

Answer Part 1

Declarer has four potential losers: three diamonds and a club. The best plan is to try to set up spades. Declarer crosses to his hand with the ♡A and leads the ♠Q which is covered with the ♠K and the ♠A. Declarer can now ruff a spade. Unfortunately, with the bad trump break, South cannot afford to ruff any more spades and is doomed to go down. This cannot be the best way to go about the spade suit. See page 74 for the second part of the answer.

HAND 15 • *To and Fro*

NORTH
♠ 7
♡ A K Q 4
♢ A 8 7 2
♣ Q J 10 4

WEST
♠ K 9 5 3 2
♡ J 8 7 2
♢ 10 4 3
♣ 5

EAST
♠ Q 8 6
♡ 10 3
♢ K 9 6 5
♣ 8 6 3 2

SOUTH
♠ A J 10 4
♡ 9 6 5
♢ Q J
♣ A K 9 7

Contract: 6♣
Opening Lead: ♣5

HAND 16 • *One Chance Only*

NORTH
♠ A K
♡ J 8 7 2
♢ K 10
♣ Q 7 6 4 3

WEST
♠ J 10 9 5
♡ A Q
♢ 5 3 2
♣ K 10 9 5

EAST
♠ 8 7 4 3
♡ 5 4 3
♢ J 9 8 6 4
♣ J

SOUTH
♠ Q 6 2
♡ K 10 9 6
♢ A Q 7
♣ A 8 2

Contract: 4♡
Opening Lead: ♠J

HAND 15 • *To and Fro*

Answer Part 1

The trump lead is not helpful. Let us say declarer wins the trick in hand and plays the ♠A and ruffs a spade. Crossing back on a trump, declarer finesses the ◇Q, losing to the ◇K, and a third trump comes back. Declarer can only come to eleven tricks this way: a spade, three hearts, five clubs and two diamonds. A better line is for declarer to finesse the ◇Q at trick two. East wins and leads a second round of trumps. South can win in hand and cash the ♠A and ruff a spade, cross back on the second diamond and ruff another spade. Now if declarer could only get back to his hand to draw trumps he would have twelve tricks but this is impossible without ruffing, which will set up a trump trick in the East hand.

Can this hand be made? See page 75 for the second part of the answer.

HAND 16 • *One Chance Only*

Answer Part 1

After North has opened 1♣, North-South arrive in 4♡. Declarer has two heart losers and one club loser (with the ♣K onside). Therefore, the only hope for the defence is for East to get a club ruff. Declarer wins ♠A and finesses a heart. Now if West returns a small club South can rise with the ♣Q. When West gets in with the ♡A he can lead a club for East to ruff, but East will be ruffing declarer's club loser. Declarer will lose only three trump tricks. Looks pretty clearcut. Are there any risks for declarer? Is there any hope for the defence? See page 75 for the second part of the answer.

SECTION 2

PRETTY DIFFICULT

HAND 17 • *What Rixi Said*

NORTH
♠ K 8
♡ 8 2
◇ K Q J 10 9
♣ A K 3 2

WEST
♠ 7 4 2
♡ 10 7 6 3
◇ 6 5 3 2
♣ 10 4

EAST
♠ A J 10
♡ K Q J 5
◇ 8 4
♣ Q J 7 5

SOUTH
♠ Q 9 6 5 3
♡ A 9 4
◇ A 7
♣ 9 8 6

W	N	E	S
	1◇	dbl	rdbl
1♡	pass	2♡	2♠
pass	3♣	pass	3◇
pass	3♠	pass	4♠
pass	pass	dbl	all pass

Contract: 4♠ doubled
Opening Lead: ♣10

HAND 18 • *The Exception*

NORTH
♠ J 9 3 2
♡ A J 9 7 3
◇ J 9 7
♣ 7

WEST
♠ K Q 10 8
♡ 5 4
◇ A 10 5
♣ A Q 4 2

EAST
♠ 6 5 4
♡ 10 6
◇ Q 6 4 2
♣ J 8 6 3

SOUTH
♠ A 7
♡ K Q 8 2
◇ K 8 3
♣ K 10 9 5

Contract: 4♡
Opening Lead: ♠K

HAND 17 • *What Rixi Said*

Answer Part 1

The late Rixi Markus used to say that most hands that are defeated can be made and many which are made could have been defeated. The hand shown here is a case in point. It is similar to a hand played by Mrs. Markus at the 1959 European Championships in Palermo.

Declarer clearly has two trump tricks to lose. He must reduce the remaining two heart losers and one club loser to one loser by ruffing or discarding them on the diamonds. The obvious approach is to draw trumps while retaining the ♡A as a stopper. For example, declarer leads the ♠K from dummy and East wins the ♠A and returns the ♡K. Declarer must duck. If East continues hearts, declarer wins the second heart and ruffs a heart, crosses to hand with the ◇A and draws trumps, playing ♠Q and another. With trumps 3-3 East is helpless to prevent declarer from throwing his club loser on the good diamonds in dummy.

But suppose after winning the ♡K East switches to the ♣Q. Now if declarer draws two more rounds of trumps, East, on gaining the lead with the ♠J, can cash a club trick. What if declarer now runs diamonds — will that work? Or perhaps declarer should not have started on trumps. Will declarer prevail or is this one for the defence? See page 75 for the second part of the answer.

HAND 18 • *The Exception*

Answer Part 1

The spade lead has been friendly but there are still problems in bringing home this ambitious game. After drawing trumps, declarer leads a spade towards dummy's ♠J. Assuming West wins this trick, he is endplayed. A spade or diamond return is fatal, and if West plays ♣A and another club to the ♣J and ♣K, declarer throws a diamond from dummy. Now declarer can set up a second diamond discard by leading the ♣10 and taking the ruffing finesse in clubs. Whether West covers or not, South can throw a second diamond on a high club and make his contract losing only a club, a diamond and a spade.

Is there some way to avoid the endplay or is there some other way to defend that will defeat this contract? See page 76 for the second part of the answer.

HAND 19 • *Mrs. Guggenheim*

NORTH
♠ Q 10
♡ A K 10 3
◇ A K J 10
♣ 7 6 4

WEST
♠ A K 9 8 5 4
♡ Q 8 2
◇ —
♣ 10 9 3 2

EAST
♠ J 7 6 3 2
♡ J 9 6 4
◇ Q 7 4 3
♣ —

SOUTH
♠ —
♡ 7 5
◇ 9 8 6 5 2
♣ A K Q J 8 5

W	N	E	S
2♠	dbl	4♠	6♣
all pass			

Contract: 6♣
Opening Lead: ♠A

HAND 20 • *A Sure Bet*

NORTH
♠ 6 3
♡ 5 3
◇ 10 9
♣ A J 10 8 6 4 2

WEST
♠ K 10 8 7
♡ 10 9 8
◇ J 8 6 4 3
♣ 3

EAST
♠ J 5 4 2
♡ K J 7 4 2
◇ 2
♣ Q 9 7

SOUTH
♠ A Q 9
♡ A Q 6
◇ A K Q 7 5
♣ K 5

Contract: 6NT
Opening Lead: ♡10

HAND 19 • *Mrs. Guggenheim*

Answer Part 1

At first glance this hand appears quite easy. However, after ruffing the opening lead and playing four rounds of trumps, discarding a heart from dummy, declarer finds that the diamond suit blockage gives him some problems.

If you throw a heart from dummy and then lead the ◇ A, ◇ K and ◇ J, East wins and you arrive at this ending.

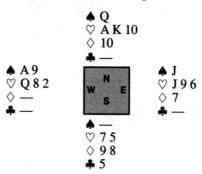

East leads a spade and the diamond suit is blocked. There are no miracles in this ending and declarer ends in dummy with an inevitable heart loser after ruffing the spade, down one.

It appears that throwing a diamond from dummy on the fourth club might help. While this does unblock the suit if East wins the third round of diamonds with the ◇ Q, if East ducks this trick declarer is in dummy with only hearts and spades and must lose two more tricks. Ruffing a spade back to hand and leading a diamond won't help since East, on winning the diamond, locks declarer in dummy by returning a heart. On the other hand, if declarer ruffs a heart back instead, the defence can simply cash a spade when they get in.

Have we missed anything? Can this hand be made? See page 77.

HAND 20 • *A Sure Bet*

Answer Part 1

Outside the club suit, declarer has only six sure tricks in his slam contract; the two top clubs make eight. If clubs are 2-2 or the ♣Q is singleton we have thirteen top tricks. But suppose the clubs don't break, as in the hand given. The obvious play is to play a small club to the ♣J at trick two . Now if East wins the ♣Q we have the rest of the tricks. But what if East ducks the ♣Q? We are back to square one. There just don't seem to be enough tricks in the side suits. To make this hand we must set up clubs and then cash them. Is there any way to do it? See page 77 for the second part of the answer.

HAND 21 • *You Have to See This*

NORTH
♠ 8 7 5 3
♡ A K
♢ Q 6
♣ Q J 9 6 5

WEST
♠ A 6
♡ J 10 8 7 4
♢ 9 4
♣ 8 4 3 2

EAST
♠ 9 2
♡ 9 2
♢ K J 10 8 7 3 2
♣ 10 7

SOUTH
♠ K Q J 10 4
♡ Q 6 5 3
♢ A 5
♣ A K

Contract: 6♠
Opening Lead: ♢ 9

HAND 22 • *An Early Warning*

NORTH
♠ A K 9 3
♡ 7 6 4
♢ 10 9 7
♣ 6 5 2

WEST
♠ Q 10 7 5 4 2
♡ Q
♢ K J 5
♣ 10 9 8

EAST
♠ J 8 6
♡ 9 8 2
♢ Q 6 4 3
♣ J 4 3

SOUTH
♠ —
♡ A K J 10 5 3
♢ A 8 2
♣ A K Q 7

Contract: 6♡
Opening Lead: ♣ 10

HAND 21 • *You Have to See This*

Answer Part 1

When this hand came up in the 1998 Canadian Team Championships, East usually pre-empted in diamonds, and West found an unpleasant lead as a result.

The 'obvious' line, which many declarers took, is to play two top hearts, cross back to hand with a club, and throw a diamond on the ♡Q. This doesn't work, of course, since East ruffs the third heart. Even without the diamond pre-empt, it's not the best line mathematically, which is to play East for at least two clubs. To do this, declarer cashes the top clubs at tricks two and three, crosses to the ♡A, and plays the ♣Q intending to get rid of his diamond loser. If East ruffs, he overruffs, crosses to the ♡K, and plays the ♣J. Again East ruffs, and South overruffs; now, however, he can play the ♡Q throwing a diamond from dummy, and East has no more trumps! Elegant, no?

But is this the last word, or can the defenders do better? See page 78 for the second part of the answer.

HAND 22 • *An Early Warning*

Answer Part 1

Declarer has three possible losers on this hand, a club and two diamonds. If trumps break there is no problem since declarer can enter dummy on a club ruff and discard the two diamonds on dummy's top spades. After two rounds of trumps, declarer tried four rounds of clubs ruffing in dummy, but East overruffed and declarer could not avoid two diamond losers. Can this hand be made? See page 78 for the second part of the answer.

HAND 23 • *Cardinal Sin*

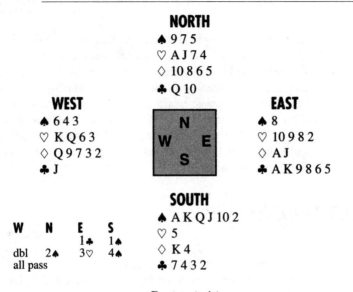

NORTH
♠ 9 7 5
♡ A J 7 4
◊ 10 8 6 5
♣ Q 10

WEST
♠ 6 4 3
♡ K Q 6 3
◊ Q 9 7 3 2
♣ J

EAST
♠ 8
♡ 10 9 8 2
◊ A J
♣ A K 9 8 6 5

SOUTH
♠ A K Q J 10 2
♡ 5
◊ K 4
♣ 7 4 3 2

W	N	E	S
		1♣	1♠
dbl	2♠	3♡	4♠
all pass			

Contract: 4♠

Opening Lead: ♣J

HAND 24 • *Helen Sobel*

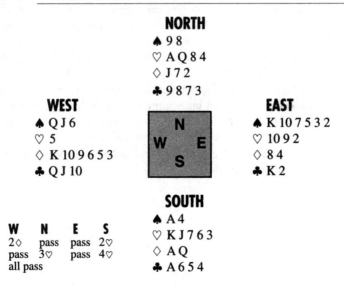

NORTH
♠ 9 8
♡ A Q 8 4
◊ J 7 2
♣ 9 8 7 3

WEST
♠ Q J 6
♡ 5
◊ K 10 9 6 5 3
♣ Q J 10

EAST
♠ K 10 7 5 3 2
♡ 10 9 2
◊ 8 4
♣ K 2

SOUTH
♠ A 4
♡ K J 7 6 3
◊ A Q
♣ A 6 5 4

W	N	E	S
2◊	pass	pass	2♡
pass	3♡	pass	4♡
all pass			

Contract: 4♡

Opening Lead: ♣Q (East plays the ♣K)

HAND 23 • *Cardinal Sin*

Answer Part 1

West leads the ♣J and East wins the trick with the ♣K. Declarer has three losers off the top: two clubs and a diamond. But to set up the South hand declarer will have to ruff two clubs in the dummy. Can declarer time it right? Continuing clubs at trick two does not seem to work for the defence on this hand since West has no high trump spots. Perhaps a trump switch is right. But when East gets in on the second club he will not have a trump to return. Is there a better defence? See page 78 for the second part of the answer.

HAND 24 • *Helen Sobel*

Answer Part 1

This famous hand (slightly modified) was played over 50 years ago at a U.S. team championship. At one table Helen Sobel, one of the greatest woman players of all time, sat South. The opening ♣Q lead was overtaken by the ♣K and both declarers won the ♣A to avoid a diamond shift. Declarer has four potential losers: two clubs, a diamond and a spade. It appears that, after drawing trumps, declarer can discard a spade on the ◇J but there are some problems. One declarer drew three rounds of trumps and then played the ◇A and ◇Q, West winning. West now shifted to a spade and declarer won and crossed to dummy on a trump to discard a spade on the ◇J. Declarer still had to give up two clubs to set up his tenth trick in the club suit. However, when the defence got in on clubs they forced declarer in spades. Now when declarer conceded the second club, he had no trumps left and the defence was able to cash a diamond.

Helen Sobel played the hand differently. See page 78 to see whether she made it.

HAND 25 • *Technical Play*

NORTH
♠ A J 5
♡ A Q
◇ 5 4 3 2
♣ 6 5 4 2

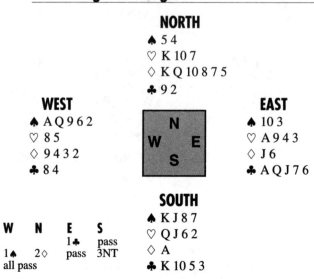

SOUTH
♠ K 10 2
♡ J 6 2
◇ A Q
♣ A Q J 10 3

W	N	E	S
			1NT
pass	3NT	all pass	

Opening Lead: ♡5

It seems best to win the ♡A to avoid a diamond shift and take the club finesse. West shows out on the first club. Now what?

HAND 26 • *Thinking It Through*

NORTH
♠ 5 4
♡ K 10 7
◇ K Q 10 8 7 5
♣ 9 2

WEST
♠ A Q 9 6 2
♡ 8 5
◇ 9 4 3 2
♣ 8 4

EAST
♠ 10 3
♡ A 9 4 3
◇ J 6
♣ A Q J 7 6

SOUTH
♠ K J 8 7
♡ Q J 6 2
◇ A
♣ K 10 5 3

W	N	E	S
		1♣	pass
1♠	2◇	pass	3NT
all pass			

Contract: 3NT
Opening Lead: ♠6

HAND 25 • *Technical Play*

Answer Part 1

You can now assure yourself of eight tricks by conceding a club trick to East. If East were to continue a heart you would have your ninth trick. But what if East switches to a diamond and West holds the ◊ K? You can still make the contract by guessing spades — but you hate to have to guess.

Is there a better way? See page 79 for the second part of the answer.

HAND 26 • *Thinking It Through*

Answer Part 1

There appears to be an adequate number of tricks on this hand, if declarer can get all of them — communication seems to be the problem. Suppose that declarer wins the opening lead with the ♠J, cashes the ◊A and continues with a heart to the king. If East ducks the ♡K, declarer must now cash diamonds reaching this ending:

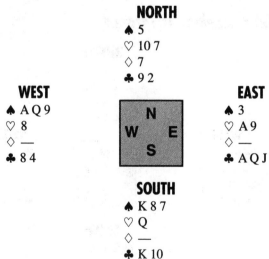

NORTH
♠ 5
♡ 10 7
◊ 7
♣ 9 2

WEST
♠ A Q 9
♡ 8
◊ —
♣ 8 4

EAST
♠ 3
♡ A 9
◊ —
♣ A Q J

SOUTH
♠ K 8 7
♡ Q
◊ —
♣ K 10

If declarer cashes the last diamond he squeezes the South hand: any card South discards allows the defence to take the rest of the tricks. If he leaves the last diamond in dummy and leads a club, East wins and continues a club to South's ♣K, the last trick for declarer. Can declarer make this hand? See page 79.

HAND 27 • *No Respect*

NORTH
♠ A 5 3
♡ Q 9
♢ 7 6 4
♣ Q J 10 7 3

WEST
♠ K
♡ A K 10 7
♢ K 10 9 5 2
♣ 8 5 2

EAST
♠ J 4
♡ J 8 6 4 2
♢ J 3
♣ K 9 6 4

SOUTH
♠ Q 10 9 8 7 6 2
♡ 5 3
♢ A Q 8
♣ A

W	N	E	S
			1♠
2♢	3♠	pass	4♠
all pass			

Contract: 4♠
Opening Lead: ♡A

HAND 28 • *Jean Besse's Hand*

NORTH
♠ Q 10
♡ A 7 5
♢ K J 9 7 6 2
♣ Q 10

WEST
♠ 9 7
♡ K J 10 9 6 2
♢ 5
♣ A 9 7 3

EAST
♠ J 5 4 3 2
♡ 4 3
♢ Q 10 3
♣ K J 2

SOUTH
♠ A K 8 6
♡ Q 8
♢ A 8 4
♣ 8 6 5 4

Contract: 3NT
Opening Lead: ♡J

HAND 27 • *No Respect*

Answer Part 1

West starts by playing the ♡A and ♡K. But what is the best continuation now? If West continues clubs or diamonds the hand is easy. But suppose West shifts to the ♠K. With the ◇K off-side, South must set up club discards to make the hand. Winning the ♠A, South crosses to his hand on the ♣A and cashes the ♠Q. Now he can cross to dummy once on the ♠5 to set up the clubs but cannot re-enter to cash them.

Is there any way to overcome this nice defence? See page 80 for the second part of the answer.

HAND 28 • *Jean Besse's Hand*

Answer Part 1

This was one of the favorite hands of the late Swiss expert Jean Besse. In a team event 3NT was the favourite contract. The South player won the opening heart lead with the ♡Q and gave up a diamond trick to East. Realizing that the best chance for the defence was in the club suit, East switched to the ♣K, and not wanting to block the suit, continued with the ♣J. However, as you can see now South's ♣8 will set up as a club stopper.

Is there any hope for the defence? See page 80 for the second part of the answer.

HAND 29 • *Give Yourself Every Chance*

NORTH
♠ Q 6
♡ A K J 9 4
◇ K 10 4
♣ 9 3 2

SOUTH
♠ A 7 3 2
♡ Q 7
◇ Q 8
♣ K J 10 8 6

W	N	E	S
			1♣
pass	1♡	pass	1♠
pass	2◇	pass	2NT
pass	3NT	all pass	

Contract: 3NT
Opening Lead: ◇7

HAND 30 • *Lucky Spots*

NORTH
♠ 9 4 3 2
♡ Q J 5 4
◇ Q J
♣ A Q 10

WEST
♠ 8 7 6 5
♡ 7 6 2
◇ K 5
♣ 5 4 3 2

EAST
♠ A J 10
♡ K 10 8 3
◇ A 6 4
♣ 8 7 6

SOUTH
♠ K Q
♡ A 9
◇ 10 9 8 7 3 2
♣ K J 9

Contract: 3NT
Opening Lead: ♠8

HAND 29 • *Give Yourself Every Chance*

Answer Part 1

A hand very similar to this one came up at IMP scoring on OkBridge, a bridge game on the Internet. This declarer was the only one to play 3NT from the wrong side. The opening lead went to the ♢4, ♢9 and ♢Q. Declarer has seven top tricks: a diamond, a spade and five hearts. You need club tricks to make the hand, so you must assume that East has the ♣Q and that if West gets in on the ♣A the defence cannot take more than three diamond tricks. Declarer ran the hearts and then played clubs, but with only one dummy entry he was not able to make two club tricks and went down. At the table, the declarer commented that it might have been better to play a heart to the nine to gain a second dummy entry. Obviously if you can get to dummy twice, you will need a less favorable lie of the club suit to make two tricks. But this line is less than 25%, even when diamonds split 4-4. Can you find the right line? See page 80 for the second part of the answer.

HAND 30 • *Lucky Spots*

Answer Part 1

East wins the opening spade lead with the ♠A. Let us assume that he continues with the ♠J, won by South with the ♠K. Declarer has a spade trick, three club tricks and a heart trick off the top. If he can set up the diamond suit, he will have nine tricks. So he leads a diamond at trick 3; say West wins and continues a spade. Even if South misguesses and rises with the ♠9, the defence can do no better than two spades and two diamonds. Can the defence do better? What if East wins the ♠A and switches to a heart, the ♡9 winning? When the defence gets in on the first diamond they can establish a heart trick, but still fall short.

Is this hand cold? See page 81 for the second part of the answer.

HAND 31 • *Step By Step*

NORTH
♠ J 10 6 3
♡ K 9 2
◇ K 5 4
♣ 9 7 5

WEST
♠ K 9 8 4 2
♡ J 6
◇ 9 8
♣ A K Q 10

EAST
♠ 7 5
♡ 10 4 3
◇ Q J 10 2
♣ 8 6 4 2

SOUTH
♠ A Q
♡ A Q 8 7 5
◇ A 7 6 3
♣ J 3

W	N	E	S
1♠	pass	pass	2♡
pass	3♡	pass	4♡
all pass			

Contract: 4♡

Opening Lead: ♣Q

HAND 32 • *It All Depends*

NORTH
♠ K J
♡ K J 10 6 2
◇ 10 7 4
♣ 7 5 2

WEST
♠ 10 8 7 6 5 2
♡ 4 3
◇ A 5
♣ 10 8 4

EAST
♠ 9 4 3
♡ Q 9 8 7
◇ K 3 2
♣ K 9 6

SOUTH
♠ A Q
♡ A 5
◇ Q J 9 8 6
♣ A Q J 3

Contract: 3NT

Opening Lead: ♠6

HAND 31 • *Step By Step*

The defence starts off with three rounds of clubs, ruffed by South. Declarer has a spade loser and two diamond losers in addition to the two clubs already lost. However, the two diamonds could be thrown on two spades. If declarer draws three rounds of trumps and plays the ♠A and ♠Q, West can duck and declarer will be left with two diamond losers. If, on the other hand, declarer does not draw trumps and plays out the ♠A and ♠Q, West can continue spades, giving his partner a chance to ruff out one of dummy's spade winners. An alternative line is to lead out the ♠Q with or without drawing trumps, but West can still duck this.

Is there any hope of making the hand? See page 81 for the second part of the answer.

HAND 32 • *It All Depends*

The spade duplication makes this 3NT contract a challenge, despite the combined 28 points of the North-South hands. Declarer has five top tricks, but setting up diamonds is hopeless after the spade lead. The obvious way to play the hand is to win the first spade in hand and play the ♡A and a heart to the jack, hoping for a favourable lie of the heart suit. As it happens, East can win the heart and clear spades. Now even though the club finesse is on, declarer cannot get back to dummy to repeat the finesse and can only take two club tricks.

Is there any way to maximize the chances and make this hand? See page 82 for the second part of the answer.

HAND 33 • *Impress the Kibitzers*

NORTH
♠ A 4 3 2
♡ 7 5 2
◇ J 10 8 3
♣ K 7

WEST
♠ Q J 10 8
♡ J 8
◇ 7 6 5 4 2
♣ Q 10

EAST
♠ K 9 7 6 5
♡ Q 10 6 4
◇ 9
♣ J 8 2

SOUTH
♠ —
♡ A K 9 3
◇ A K Q
♣ A 9 6 5 4 3

Contract: 6♣
Opening Lead: ♠Q

HAND 34 • *Raising the Dead*

NORTH
♠ Q 10 6
♡ 6 5 3
◇ J 6 5 2
♣ K Q 7

W	N	E	S
			2♣
pass	2◇	pass	2♡
pass	3♡	pass	4♣
pass	4♡	pass	6♡
all pass			

SOUTH
♠ A K 2
♡ A K Q 10 9 7
◇ A K 7 4
♣ —

Contract: 6♡
Opening Lead: ◇3

HAND 33 • *Impress the Kibitzers*

Answer Part 1

To have any chance to make this hand, declarer needs a 3-2 trump break. Declarer still has two heart losers. One can go on the ♠A. The second heart could go on the long diamond but declarer must unblock the diamonds in his hand by cashing three rounds of diamonds before drawing trumps, hoping for a 3-3 diamond break. This hand was played by a local expert who decided to improve his chances; he had seen a similar hand in Terence Reese's famous book *Play Bridge with Reese*. He won the ♠A and threw away the ◇A, which certainly impressed the kibitzers. He now crossed to his hand on the ♣A and led the top two diamonds from his hand. East showed out but didn't ruff. Now when declarer crossed to the ♣K and led the third diamond, East ruffed and declarer was left with a heart loser.

Can you do better? See page 82 for the second part of the answer.

HAND 34 • *Raising the Dead*

Answer Part 1

Declarer draws trumps and tries diamonds. If the diamond suit splits 3-2, or if the ◇Q is singleton or if the ◇Q is held by West the hand is easy: South gives up a diamond and the hand is cold. But unfortunately, it turns out that West has a singleton diamond. Declarer could enter dummy with the ♠Q and run the ♣K discarding a diamond, but when the defence wins the ♣A declarer cannot return to dummy to cash the remaining club winner.

Is there a better plan? When you draw trumps, West has three and East has one. See page 82 for the second part of the answer.

HAND 35 • *A Rare Ending*

NORTH
♠ K 6 5 4
♡ 8 7 3
◇ 9 6 3
♣ J 9 3

WEST
♠ 10 9 8
♡ 9 6 2
◇ 5 4 2
♣ Q 10 8 2

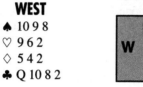

EAST
♠ A Q J 3 2
♡ J 4
◇ 10 8 7
♣ A 6 5

SOUTH
♠ 7
♡ A K Q 10 5
◇ A K Q J
♣ K 7 4

W	N	E	S
		1♠	dbl
pass	1NT	pass	3♡
pass	4♡	all pass	

Contract: 4♡

Opening Lead: ♠10

HAND 36 • *Play It Safe*

NORTH
♠ A 8 7 4 3
♡ K 8
◇ J 6 5
♣ Q J 9

WEST
♠ 5
♡ 7 6 3
◇ A K Q 9 8 4
♣ 10 8 6

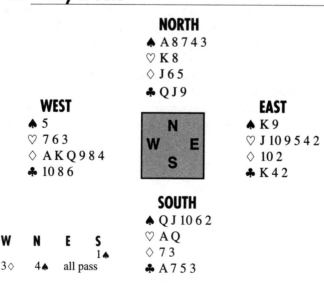

EAST
♠ K 9
♡ J 10 9 5 4 2
◇ 10 2
♣ K 4 2

SOUTH
♠ Q J 10 6 2
♡ A Q
◇ 7 3
♣ A 7 5 3

W	N	E	S
			1♠
3◇	4♠	all pass	

Contract: 4♠

Opening Lead: ◇K

HAND 35 • *A Rare Ending*

Answer Part 1

After declarer ducks the opening spade lead, West continues with another spade. South has one spade loser and with hearts behaving, he needs to hold his club losers to two. After drawing three rounds of trumps, South should play off his top three diamonds. Now his faint hope is to find East with the ♣AQ and West with the ♣10. Then he can play a club to the ♣9 and ♣Q. Ruffing the ♠A, declarer gives up the ♣A, establishing his club winner. But as we can see this won't work, since West can rise on the ♣Q and lead another spade through, declarer ruffing. Now declarer cannot establish a club trick since when East wins the ♣A, he has a good spade to cash.

Is there a better way? See page 83 for the second part of the answer.

HAND 36 • *Play It Safe*

Answer Part 1

The best approach for the defence is to start off with three top diamonds. East discards a heart and South ruffs. Declarer has four potential losers: two diamonds, a club and a spade. If declarer finesses the spade, East will win and can get out safely with a spade or a heart. Now declarer will have to lose a club at some point in the hand. But what if declarer plays a spade to the ace? After all, West can hardly have the ♠K too considering his pre-empt.

Is there an endplay possible? See page 83 for the second part of the answer.

HAND 37 • *There Is a Way*

NORTH
♠ 6
♡ 8 6 4 2
◇ K Q J 9 4 2
♣ K 6

WEST
♠ 5 3 2
♡ A K 7 5 3
◇ 6 5 3
♣ A Q

	N	
W		E
	S	

EAST
♠ 10 8
♡ Q J 10
◇ A 8 7
♣ 10 7 4 3 2

SOUTH
♠ A K Q J 9 7 4
♡ 9
◇ 10
♣ J 9 8 5

W	N	E	S
1♡	2◇	2♡	4♠
all pass			

Contract: 4♠
Opening Lead: ♡K

HAND 38 • *Last Chance*

NORTH
♠ K J 5
♡ 9 7 6
◇ K
♣ Q 10 7 6 4 3

WEST
♠ Q 9 3
♡ Q 2
◇ J 10 9 7 4 2
♣ A K

	N	
W		E
	S	

EAST
♠ A 8 6 4
♡ 10 8 5 3
◇ 8 3
♣ 9 5 2

SOUTH
♠ 10 7 2
♡ A K J 4
◇ A Q 6 5
♣ J 8

Contract: 3NT
Opening Lead: ◇J

HAND 37 • *There Is a Way*

Answer Part 1

Declarer has three top losers — a heart, a diamond and a club. However, declarer could have two more club losers. With the lucky lie of the club suit, declarer's ♣J sets up. Declarer can discard his other club on a diamond winner after forcing out the ♢A.

What if West switches to ♣A and ♣Q? Does that cause South any difficulties? Can this hand be made? See page 84 for the second part of the answer.

HAND 38 • *Last Chance*

Answer Part 1

After winning the ♢K, declarer has five red-suit tricks on top, and can set up four additional tricks in clubs. Starting on clubs immediately he leads a club to the ♣J and the ♣K. Seeing no future in diamonds, West shifts to the ♠3. Whether East wins the ♠A or ducks, the defence is helpless.

Can you see any way to defeat this contract? See page 84 for the second part of the answer.

HAND 39 • *A Meagre Clue*

NORTH
♠ K 2
♡ A Q 8 4 3
♢ K 8 3
♣ Q 7 5

SOUTH
♠ A 8
♡ K 10 9 7 2
♢ Q 5 4
♣ A 8 6

Contract: 4♡

Opening Lead: ♠J

HAND 40 • *A Lucky Mistake*

NORTH
♠ K 10 5
♡ J 10 8
♢ 8
♣ A J 7 6 4 2

WEST
♠ J 7 2
♡ A K
♢ K J 7 6 5 2
♣ 9 8

EAST
♠ Q 8 6 4
♡ 6 4
♢ 9 4 3
♣ K Q 10 5

SOUTH
♠ A 9 3
♡ Q 9 7 5 3 2
♢ A Q 10
♣ 3

W	N	E	S
			1♡
2♢	4♡	all pass	

Contract: 4♡

Opening Lead: ♡A

HAND 39 • *A Meagre Clue*

Answer Part 1

Declarer has four potential losers: two diamonds and two clubs. If West has the ♣K all is well since declarer can hold his club losers to one. Are there any other chances? If one hand has the doubleton ◇A, declarer can hold the diamond losers to one, if he guesses which defender has that holding. There is one other chance: if declarer could end up with East on lead after drawing trumps and eliminating spades and diamonds, the contract would be assured. Declarer wins the ♠K and draws trumps, West having three trumps.

Can you see the best line now? See page 84 for the second part of the answer.

HAND 40 • *A Lucky Mistake*

Answer Part 1

The best start for the defence appears to be cashing the top hearts and shifting to a club won by North with the ♣A. At this point declarer has a potential spade loser and a diamond loser. One possibility is to establish clubs. Declarer can win the ♣A and ruff a club, and with two entries to dummy can make the hand if clubs are 3-3 (but as we can see, clubs don't split) — this combined with the spade finesse seems to be pretty good odds — but it looks like the hand is doomed to defeat.

Can you see any other possibilities in this hand — a squeeze, an endplay? Should the defence start out differently? See page 85 for the second part of the answer.

SECTION 3

REALLY
CHALLENGING

HAND 41 • *Handling Charges*

NORTH
- ♠ Q J 10 7 2
- ♡ J 9 5 3 2
- ◇ 4
- ♣ Q 4

WEST
- ♠ 9 3
- ♡ A 10 6 4
- ◇ 5 3
- ♣ K 10 7 5 2

EAST
- ♠ A 6 5 4
- ♡ —
- ◇ A J 10 9 7
- ♣ J 8 6 3

SOUTH
- ♠ K 8
- ♡ K Q 8 7
- ◇ K Q 8 6 2
- ♣ A 9

W	N	E	S
	pass	1◇	1NT
pass	2♣	pass	2♡
pass	4♡	pass	pass
dbl	all pass		

Contract: 4♡ doubled

Opening Lead: ◇5

HAND 42 • *The Crane Hand*

NORTH
- ♠ 8 5 3 2
- ♡ J 6 2
- ◇ 8 5
- ♣ 8 5 3 2

WEST
- ♠ J 10 9 4
- ♡ A 10 9
- ◇ 9 7 6 4
- ♣ 9 7

EAST
- ♠ Q 7 6
- ♡ K 4
- ◇ A Q 10 3 2
- ♣ 10 6 4

SOUTH
- ♠ A K
- ♡ Q 8 7 5 3
- ◇ K J
- ♣ A K Q J

Contract: 4♡

Opening Lead: ♠J

HAND 41 • *Handling Charges*

Answer Part 1

This hand was played in the World Junior Team Championships in Hamilton, Ontario in 1997. East wins the ◇A and switches to a club. As we can see, declarer must win the ♣A and play a top diamond shedding his ♣Q. It seems natural to lay down a top heart, West winning and returning a high club which is ruffed. Let's say that declarer now plays spades. East will duck the first round and win the second round. If East continues a third spade, South has to ruff high. Declarer is left with the ♡7 and ♡8 in hand. West covers the ♡8 with the ♡10. This effectively blocks the heart suit and declarer cannot return to dummy to draw trumps without reducing dummy's trump holding and establishing West's ♡6 as the long trump. Is there any way around this weird blockage in the trump suit? Is this the best defence? See page 85 for the second part of the answer.

HAND 42 • *The Crane Hand*

Answer Part 1

There are two potential diamond losers and at least two heart losers in this hand. One requirement is that declarer must be able to get to dummy to lead toward the diamond tenace to hold the diamond losers to one. That will require a favourable lie of the heart suit. Another challenge is to hold the heart losers to two. South recalled a similar hand played some time ago by the late Barry Crane. Crane found the best chance to limit his trump losers to two. Declarer starts off with the ♡Q. This will allow him to hold the trump losers to two if West has the doubleton ♡AK or if East has either the doubleton ♡A or ♡K. South's plan is next to lead up to the ♡J in dummy. East wins the ♡K and exits a black suit, and on the lie of the cards declarer is home. Winning the return, declarer leads another trump towards dummy. Whether West wins or ducks, South cannot be prevented from entering dummy to lead towards the diamonds in his hand and West cannot score more than one more heart trick. Can the defence come up with another strategy? See page 86 for the second part of the answer.

HAND 43 • *At the World Championships*

NORTH
♠ A K
♡ K 9 5
◇ Q J 10 8 3
♣ 8 6 4

WEST
♠ Q 9 4 2
♡ J
◇ K 9 6 5
♣ K 10 5 3

EAST
♠ 10
♡ 8 7 6 3
◇ A 2
♣ A Q J 9 7 2

W	N	E	S
		2♣¹	2♡
4♣	4♡	all pass	

1. 11-15 HCP and either 6+♣ or 5♣ and a 4-card major.

SOUTH
♠ J 8 7 6 5 3
♡ A Q 10 4 2
◇ 7 4
♣ —

Contract: 4♡

Opening Lead: ♣3

HAND 44 • *Perfection?*

NORTH
♠ A 9 8 2
♡ Q 10 9
◇ A Q 2
♣ J 10 5

WEST
♠ 3
♡ K 3 2
◇ 9 7 5 4 3
♣ Q 9 8 2

EAST
♠ Q J 7 6 4
♡ J
◇ K J 8
♣ A 7 6 3

SOUTH
♠ K 10 5
♡ A 8 7 6 5 4
◇ 10 6
♣ K 4

W	N	E	S
	1♣	1♠	2♡
pass	3♡	pass	4♡
all pass			

Contract: 4♡

Opening Lead: ♠3

HAND 43 • *At the World Championships*

When this hand was played at the 1996 Bridge Olympiad in Rhodes, the French declarer knew a lot about the distribution from the bidding. After ruffing the club lead, declarer must set up either diamonds or spades since a cross-ruff is unlikely to produce enough tricks and in fact on the actual distribution will fail. Suppose that declarer starts by cashing the top spades; East will ruff in, and the best defence now is a trump. There do not seem to be enough entries to establish the spade suit. If declarer tries to establish diamonds the defence can continue clubs and ruff South down. The Vu-Graph commentators decided the hand could not be made. Were they right? See page 87 for the second part of the answer.

HAND 44 • *Perfection?*

This hand was played during an exhibition match on OkBridge. The East-West pair were Bobby Goldman and Paul Soloway, both world champions. You can be sure that they made no mistakes on defence. The spade lead went to the ♠2, ♠J and ♠K. Declarer has a likely heart loser, a diamond loser, a spade loser and at least one club loser. However, the diamond can be discarded on dummy's fourth spade. So declarer led the ♡A and another heart, won by Goldman with the ♡K. Now it is true that Goldman can lead a club to Soloway's ♣A and receive a spade ruff. But then if Goldman returns a diamond, declarer wins the ♢A, cashes the ♡Q, crosses to hand on the ♣K and runs hearts, and Soloway is squeezed in diamonds and spades. If Goldman returns a club, declarer wins, cashes the ♡Q and the ♢A and ruffs a club to hand and proceeds on similar lines.

But what if Goldman plays a diamond instead of a club when he is in on the ♡K? What then? See page 88 for the second part of the answer.

HAND 45 • *A Good Idea*

NORTH
♠ A J 10
♡ A 8 7 5
◇ Q J
♣ 9 7 4 3

WEST
♠ K Q 8 7 5 2
♡ 10
◇ K 7 4
♣ K J 10

EAST
♠ 9 6 4 3
♡ 2
◇ 10 8 6 5 3 2
♣ 6 5

SOUTH
♠ —
♡ K Q J 9 6 4 3
◇ A 9
♣ A Q 8 2

W	N	E	S
1♠	pass	pass	4♡
pass	6♡	all pass	

Contract: 6♡

Opening Lead: ♠K

HAND 46 • *A Master At Play*

NORTH
♠ Q J
♡ A J 7 2
◇ J 9 4
♣ A K 10 9

WEST
♠ 9 5 4 2
♡ 10 9 5
◇ K Q 2
♣ 6 5 2

EAST
♠ 7
♡ K Q 8 6
◇ A 10 6 5 3
♣ Q 8 4

SOUTH
♠ A K 10 8 6 3
♡ 4 3
◇ 8 7
♣ J 7 3

Contract: 4♠

Opening Lead: ◇ K

HAND 45 • *A Good Idea*

Answer Part 1

Declarer has four potential losers in the South hand, a diamond and three clubs, and only one discard on the ♠A. Since West is marked on the auction with the outstanding high cards, South cannot rely on any finesses working. Winning the opening spade lead with the ♠A, South needs to find some sort of endplay on the West hand. Suppose South discards a club on the ♠A and eliminates the spade suit by ruffing a spade, crossing back to dummy on the trump ace, and ruffing the last spade. Now South can continue with the ◇A and ◇Q. West is in and is endplayed — but whether West returns a spade, diamond or club, South can only get rid of one club loser and will still have another club loser. With so many high cards in the West hand perhaps some sort of squeeze, or squeeze and endplay, is in order? Perhaps declarer should discard a diamond on the ♠A. One trick is not enough; to prevail declarer must manufacture two tricks.

Can this hand be made? See page 89 for the second part of the answer.

HAND 46 • *A Master At Play*

Answer Part 1

This hand was played by Belladonna against Wolff and Jacoby in the finals of the 1973 World Championships. Jacoby led the ◇K, cashed a second diamond and shifted to the ♡10; dummy played the ♡J and Wolff won the deceptive ♡K. Wolff now continued a third diamond ruffed by declarer. It looked like the Americans had found the perfect defence. Even looking at all the cards, there seems no clear way to make ten tricks. Perhaps there is a squeeze...

You could cash the top clubs and run the trumps. The ♣J would be a menace against East but unfortunately West can guard hearts. If you ruff out West's heart guard, you will not be able to cash the top clubs, though.

Can the master find a way? Was this really the best start for the defence? See page 89 for the second part of the answer.

HAND 47 • *A Strange Endplay*

NORTH
♠ J 6 2
♡ K 10 6 4
◇ K 10
♣ Q 9 8 2

WEST
♠ A Q 8 7 5
♡ 8
◇ 8 4 3
♣ A K 5 3

EAST
♠ 10 9
♡ 9 7 2
◇ 7 6 5
♣ J 10 7 6 4

SOUTH
♠ K 4 3
♡ A Q J 5 3
◇ A Q J 9 2
♣ —

W	N	E	S
			1♡
2♡	dbl	3♣	3◇
pass	4♡	pass	6♡
all pass			

Contract: 6♡

Opening Lead: ♣A

HAND 48 • *Smothered*

NORTH
♠ K Q
♡ A 7 2
◇ J 9 7
♣ A 10 8 5 3

WEST
♠ 10 4 3 2
♡ K Q J
◇ 8 6 5 4
♣ 7 4

EAST
♠ J
♡ 10 9 8 6 5 4
◇ 10 3 2
♣ Q J 6

SOUTH
♠ A 9 8 7 6 5
♡ 3
◇ A K Q
♣ K 9 2

Contract: 6♠

Opening Lead: ♡K

HAND 47 • *A Strange Endplay*

This interesting hand is similar to one reported from far-away Bulgaria, in a teams competition. Both tables reached 6♡, after West had shown the black suits. Declarer has two spade losers on the lie of the cards. One option is to discard dummy's spades on declarer's long diamonds. Suppose declarer plays three rounds of trumps and then runs five diamonds, discarding all of dummy's spades. Now declarer can ruff only one spade in dummy. West will be under some pressure on the run of the diamonds but he can keep three spades and one club as his last four cards. This is the ending, and West cannot be prevented from taking the second defensive trick.

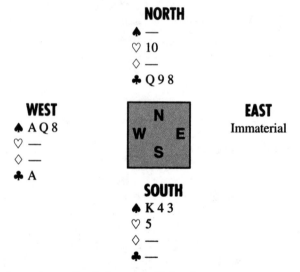

NORTH
♠ —
♡ 10
◇ —
♣ Q 9 8

WEST
♠ A Q 8
♡ —
◇ —
♣ A

EAST
Immaterial

SOUTH
♠ K 4 3
♡ 5
◇ —
♣ —

Is there a better line? See page 90 for the answer.

HAND 48 • *Smothered*

After winning the opening lead with the ♡A, declarer cashed the ♠K and saw the ♠J on his right. If the spades break the slam is cold since South has only a club loser. But if you believe the ♠J is a true card, as it is, then prospects are looking poor. It appears that South must play the club suit for no losers — which does not work on this hand. If you are confident that the ♠J is a true card, is there an alternative line that will make the hand on this lie of the cards? See page 92 for the second part of the answer.

HAND 49 • *The Moysian Fit*

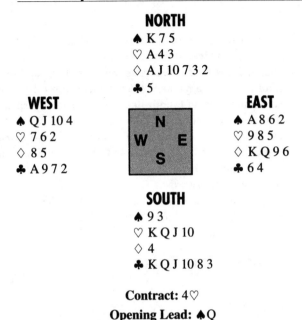

NORTH
♠ K 7 5
♡ A 4 3
◇ A J 10 7 3 2
♣ 5

WEST
♠ Q J 10 4
♡ 7 6 2
◇ 8 5
♣ A 9 7 2

EAST
♠ A 8 6 2
♡ 9 8 5
◇ K Q 9 6
♣ 6 4

SOUTH
♠ 9 3
♡ K Q J 10
◇ 4
♣ K Q J 10 8 3

Contract: 4♡

Opening Lead: ♠Q

HAND 50 • *At the Blue Ribbon*

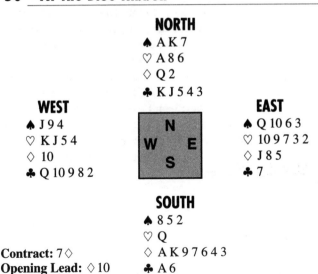

NORTH
♠ A K 7
♡ A 8 6
◇ Q 2
♣ K J 5 4 3

WEST
♠ J 9 4
♡ K J 5 4
◇ 10
♣ Q 10 9 8 2

EAST
♠ Q 10 6 3
♡ 10 9 7 3 2
◇ J 8 5
♣ 7

SOUTH
♠ 8 5 2
♡ Q
◇ A K 9 7 6 4 3
♣ A 6

Contract: 7◇
Opening Lead: ◇ 10

This hand was played in the 1996 Blue Ribbon Pairs in Atlanta, and no-one made the grand slam. After drawing three rounds of trumps, not being clairvoyant, you try ♣A and a club to the king, East showing out. Can you make the hand from here?

HAND 49 • *The Moysian Fit*

Answer Part 1

Playing on a 4-3 fit is often a challenge. On this hand the defence starts with three rounds of spades and South is forced to shorten himself at trick three since, with three top losers, he can't afford to duck anything. Now declarer must establish his long suit while keeping trumps in dummy to handle a spade continuation, so it is clear to start clubs immediately. West wins the ♣A and continues with spades anyway, hoping to cause declarer some difficulties in the trump suit. However, South can ruff and with trumps 3-3 can still make his contract. This hand seems pretty straightforward.

Can you see a way for the defence to make it more of a challenge? Should this hand be made? See page 92 for the second part of the answer.

HAND 50 • *At the Blue Ribbon*

Answer Part 1

You have twelve top tricks, two spades, one heart, two clubs and seven diamonds, and the thirteenth is going to have to come from some sort of squeeze. One possibility is a double squeeze with hearts as the central suit. In this squeeze, declarer cashes the top spades and then runs diamonds, East has to guard spades and West clubs, forcing both defenders to discard hearts. Unfortunately, for this to work West must be unable to guard spades. On the lie of the cards with West holding three spades to the jack this squeeze won't work. Likewise a spade-club squeeze against West won't work. Somehow we have to get the heart suit into play. If the ace and queen of hearts were exchanged, we could squeeze West in hearts and clubs. What about some kind of trump squeeze? Perhaps this hand cannot be made on best defence...See page 94 for the second part of the answer.

HAND 51 • *A Classic Deal*

NORTH
♠ Q 10 9 5 2
♡ 10 9 7
♢ K 10
♣ A 9 7

WEST
♠ K
♡ K Q J 4
♢ A Q 9 6 4 3
♣ Q 4

EAST
♠ —
♡ A 8 5 2
♢ J 8 7 5 2
♣ K 10 8 2

SOUTH
♠ A J 8 7 6 4 3
♡ 6 3
♢ —
♣ J 6 5 3

W	N	E	S
1♢	pass	1♡	1♠
3♡	3♠	4♢	pass
4♡	4♠	all pass	

Contract: 4♠

Opening Lead: ♡K

HAND 52 • *A Sweet Ending*

NORTH
♠ Q J
♡ 9 7
♢ Q 7 6 5 2
♣ A 10 9 8

WEST
♠ 8
♡ Q 3 2
♢ K J 10 4 3
♣ K 5 4 2

EAST
♠ A 10 4
♡ A J 10 5 4
♢ A 8
♣ J 6 3

SOUTH
♠ K 9 7 6 5 3 2
♡ K 8 6
♢ 9
♣ Q 7

W	N	E	S
	pass	1♡	1♠
2♡	dbl	3♡	3♠
all pass			

Contract: 3♠

Opening Lead: ♡2

HAND 51 • *A Classic Deal*

Answer Part 1

After winning the ♡K, let us assume that West continues a heart to the ace and then East plays a third heart, ruffed by declarer. Now it seems right for declarer to cross to dummy with a trump and eliminate the diamond suit before tackling clubs. On the bidding, West is marked with a doubleton club; knowing this, can declarer play the clubs for one loser? Perhaps there is an endplay. Is this the right line for the defence? Perhaps they have not found their best line, even at trick 2 or 3? See page 95 for the second part of the answer.

HAND 52 • *A Sweet Ending*

Answer Part 1

When this hand was played in an IMP Pairs game at a local club, between two top-notch pairs, East won the ♡A and had to decide what to play next. If East continues hearts, declarer has the entries to ruff out East's ◇A setting up a simple minor-suit squeeze on West. South will win the ♡K and duck a diamond, West winning. Now, whatever West plays, South has an entry to dummy to play a second diamond. For example, if West continues hearts, South ruffs; this promotes a second trump trick for the defence but South can continue with a diamond, ruffing out East's ◇A. Since the defence can never attack clubs, South can now make the hand by squeezing West in diamonds and clubs: he simply gives up the two spade tricks to East and runs his spades. This is the ending with the defence having won three tricks as South leads the last spade:

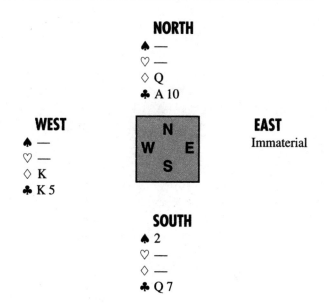

NORTH
♠ —
♡ —
◇ Q
♣ A 10

WEST
♠ —
♡ —
◇ K
♣ K 5

EAST
Immaterial

SOUTH
♠ 2
♡ —
◇ —
♣ Q 7

And West is history.

At the table, East continued ♠ A and another spade at tricks 2 and 3, prematurely knocking out a dummy entry. Declarer won in dummy and led a diamond from dummy (which East must duck to avoid the squeeze), West winning. West now returned a heart, South winning with the ♡ K.

Has the defence picked its way through the minefield or can declarer find a way home anyway? And if so, could the defenders have done better? See page 96 for the second part of the answer.

ANSWERS PART 2

HAND 1 • *Extra Chance*

The correct way to play this hand is to establish a second entry to the South hand by overtaking the ♠K with the ♠A at trick one. Now declarer leads up to dummy's clubs, then draws trumps ending in hand and then leads towards dummy's clubs again. As the cards lie, if West ducks for a second time, declarer can go up with the ♣K and, having avoided the unavoidable club loser, can now simply give up a heart. If West rises, declarer will find himself with two winning clubs on which to pitch the hearts in hand. Of course if the ♣J did not come down in three rounds as it does in this particular hand, declarer could ruff the last club and fall back on the heart finesse. If we were not looking at all four hands it would not be clear to play West for the ♣A if he ducked twice. Any good East should duck the first club with the ♣A, assuming West gives count when the first club is led. But unless the West has the ♣A, we shall not be able to establish the required three club winners and the heart finesse will be our only recourse — so we may as well play for this helpful club distribution.

HAND 2 • *On Your Toes*

This hand *can* be made. Declarer's goal is to avoid letting West in on lead to give his partner a club ruff. Declarer first cashes the ♢A and then as before cashes the ♡A. But now instead of a second heart, declarer leads dummy's ♢Q, and when East covers with the ♢K declarer throws his ♠J. This loser-on-loser play forces East to win the second defensive trick. Now it is impossible for the defence to get West on lead for the club ruff. Whatever East returns, declarer will win it and force out the ♡K and eventually draw trumps, holding the defence to three tricks: a spade, a diamond and the ♡K.

HAND 3 • *Safety Play*

There is a 100% line that guarantees twelve tricks. Declarer crosses to dummy on the ♡A and leads the ♠J to take the proven finesse in spades. If East covers he crosses back on the ♠10 and ruffs a heart. If East ducks the spade he ruffs a heart and then cashes another top spade. Either way, he arrives at the same position. South then crosses to dummy on the ◇K and ruffs the ◇J, eliminating the red suits and arriving at this position:

NORTH
♠ 6
♡ —
◇ —
♣ 9 6 4 3

SOUTH
♠ 9
♡ —
◇ —
♣ A K J 2

Now he cashes the ♣A and leads a club to dummy's ♣9. If clubs are 3-2 he has the rest of the tricks, if East has four clubs he can win the ♣10 but will be forced either to lead another club which South can finesse or give declarer a ruff-sluff. If West has the four clubs he too will be endplayed and must lead a club into declarer's tenace or give up a ruff-sluff. This was the only way to make the hand since the whole hand was:

NORTH
♠ J 10 6 2
♡ A Q
♢ K J 5
♣ 9 6 4 3

WEST
♠ —
♡ J 8 5 4 2
♢ 10 9 8 3
♣ Q 10 8 5

```
       N
   W       E
       S
```

EAST
♠ Q 7 3
♡ K 10 9 6 3
♢ Q 7 6 2
♣ 7

SOUTH
♠ A K 9 8 5 4
♡ 7
♢ A 4
♣ A K J 2

HAND 4 • *Routine*

This hand *should not* be made. East must get his partner in for another lead through dummy's diamonds. West can hardly have much more than a jack or two. East's best chance is to play his partner for the ♣J. The first three tricks go the same way as described in Part 1, but when declarer crosses to dummy on the second spade, East must jettison the ♣A! West must eventually get in with the ♣J (or declarer only has eight tricks) and can lead a diamond through dummy's ♢Qx to defeat the contract.

HAND 5 • *Elementary, My Dear Watson*

Holmes realized that the diamond finesse is not really an additional chance to make the hand: if West has the ♢K, East must have the ♠K since West passed originally. So any time the finesse of the ♢K works, it is unnecessary, since the spade finesse also works! Another choice is to lead a diamond and play the ten. This wins whenever West has the ♢J, since even if you lose to the ♢K, you will have two pitches for your spades.

Sherlock Holmes, however, led a diamond to dummy's ♢A at trick two and continued with the ♢Q. When it was covered with the ◇K, he had learned the location of one of the missing kings. If West had produced the ◇K, Holmes would have known that the ♠K was well placed; sadly, since East had the ◇K, the great man was still no wiser regarding the location of the ♠K. There were still some extra chances however. Holmes next played a trump to the queen and led a small diamond from dummy — when the ◇J appeared on his right, he was home.

"But what if the ◇J had not fallen?" said his partner.

"Then I would have crossed to dummy and led the ◇10. I discard a spade if it is not covered, endplaying West if he has the ◇J. If East covers the ◇10 I shall ruff and finally be forced to cross to dummy in hearts one more time to take the spade finesse — about a 90% line."

"Wonderful play!"

"Elementary, my dear Watson."

The full hand was:

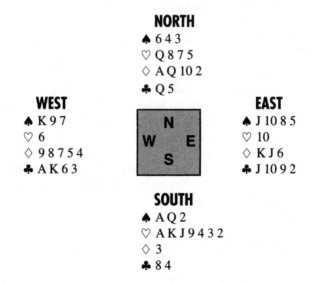

NORTH
♠ 6 4 3
♡ Q 8 7 5
◇ A Q 10 2
♣ Q 5

WEST
♠ K 9 7
♡ 6
◇ 9 8 7 5 4
♣ A K 6 3

EAST
♠ J 10 8 5
♡ 10
◇ K J 6
♣ J 10 9 2

SOUTH
♠ A Q 2
♡ A K J 9 4 3 2
◇ 3
♣ 8 4

While it is true that merely ruffing two diamonds will allow you to make contract as well, since the ◇KJ are tripleton, this is a much better line. So you need to follow the great man's solution for full marks.

HAND 6 • *When The Going Gets Tough, the Tough Take a Finesse*

There are several lines that might be tried on this hand. Overtaking the ◇K doesn't quite work since South gets left with the ◇10 as a loser when the smoke clears; similarly a ruffing finesse in clubs fails since West has the ♣A. The line that seems best (and works on the actual hand) is to win the second trump and cash the ♡K. Declarer then leads a small club and ruffs it. Now he cashes the ♡A and ruffs a heart. If hearts break declarer can draw the last trump and claim. But if hearts don't break declarer still has another chance: he finesses the ◇10! This provides an extra entry to the South hand. Now declarer can ruff a second heart, cross back to hand by overtaking the ◇K with the ◇A, draw the last trump and run the established heart suit.

HAND 7 • *About Finesses*

This hand is cold on the lie of the cards, using a Morton's Fork Coup. After winning the opening lead and drawing trumps, declarer leads a heart from dummy. East is caught on the horns of a dilemma; if he rises with the ♡K, declarer now has two heart tricks (the ♡Q and the ♡10) and can discard dummy's club loser on South's winning heart. So East must duck and South wins the ♡10. Now declarer endplays West, eliminating diamonds, cashing the ♣A and throwing West in by leading the ♣Q. Now with only one heart remaining in dummy, when West presents South with a ruff-sluff, South throws dummy's losing heart and makes the hand.

HAND 8 • *Numero Uno*

Bob Hamman, the top rated bridge player in the World Bridge Federation rankings, made this hand. After drawing trumps and cashing hearts, Hamman led the ♠J at trick 7 but when West played the ♠Q, Bob ducked in dummy! West's best play is to continue spades to dummy's ♠K and East's ♠A. But now East is endplayed — he has no more spades and must either lead a diamond (establishing dummy's ◇J as an entry) or a club (putting declarer in dummy to cash the remaining three club tricks). (You can also lead the ♠9 at trick 7 as long as you do not play the ♠K from dummy until trick 8). The defence cannot attack spades themselves without giving you a trick so the hand will always make as the cards lie. The whole hand was:

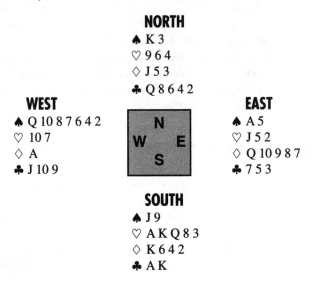

NORTH
♠ K 3
♡ 9 6 4
◇ J 5 3
♣ Q 8 6 4 2

WEST
♠ Q 10 8 7 6 4 2
♡ 10 7
◇ A
♣ J 10 9

EAST
♠ A 5
♡ J 5 2
◇ Q 10 9 8 7
♣ 7 5 3

SOUTH
♠ J 9
♡ A K Q 8 3
◇ K 6 4 2
♣ A K

HAND 9 • *The Forcing Defence*

After the fourth club the hand cannot be made. Declarer ruffs small on the board but East discards a heart on the third club, and gets rid of his second heart on the fourth club. Now declarer can lead the ♠J and another spade but has no entry to dummy to repeat the spade finesse a third time.

HAND 10 • *Trump Promotion*

This hand can be made with a loser-on-loser play. South ruffs a spade in dummy and plays the third round of diamonds himself, throwing his club loser. East can win but since he has no more diamonds he cannot promote a second trump trick in West's hand.

HAND 11 • *The Right Hand*

After West shows out in spades, it is apparent that declarer's best chance to make the contract is to score three diamond tricks. Therefore, South should win the second round of spades in dummy with the ♠A and lead the ◇J, covered by East and won with the ◇A. Declarer continues spades until East wins the ♠K and returns a heart to dummy's ♡A as before. But now after running spades, South can play a diamond to the ◇9 which wins, for his ninth trick.

HAND 12 • *Know Your Odds*

South can play the odds and this hand can be made. Declarer does not need three spade tricks, if he can achieve five club tricks. South should win the first trick in hand by overtaking the ♠Q with the ♠K. Now he runs the ♣Q and can return to hand safely with the ♡A for a second club play. All in all, he will take two spade tricks, two heart tricks, three diamond tricks, and five club tricks.

HAND 13 • *A Failed Effort*

The hand is cold but not the way declarer played it. When declarer cashes the ◇A, West should jettison the ◇K creating an entry to the East hand to cash the long heart. But declarer can thwart this play — he simply does not cash the ◇A! He leads a diamond towards dummy at trick two and plays the ◇Q if West ducks. South then continues by leading another diamond from dummy and when East plays the ◇9, South ducks. West must win the ◇K and the suit is established without giving East the lead.

HAND 14 • *Your Long Suit*

This hand can be made. Declarer can afford to give up a spade trick and should do so immediately. Winning the ♣A, declarer should lead a spade to the ♠Q and West's ♠K. Winning the club return, declarer can cash the ♡Q and ruff a spade high. Declarer then draws trumps and since the spades have broken 4-2 they are now good. Declarer can cross to dummy on the ◇A to cash his four winning spades, making his contract with four spade tricks, five heart tricks, a diamond and two clubs.

HAND 15 • *To and Fro*

Declarer can make this hand if he manages his entries properly. Winning the opening lead in hand declarer starts by playing the ♠A and ruffing a spade. Then declarer leads a diamond from the dummy; East wins and plays a trump, won in hand. Now declarer ruffs one more spade and crosses back to hand with the ◇Q to draw trumps. Declarer has twelve tricks: three hearts, one spade, two diamonds and six trump tricks. Declarer cannot waste a hand entry to take the unnecessary diamond finesse.

HAND 16 • *One Chance Only*

This hand can be defeated. Perhaps West can determine from the auction that his one chance is to score a club trick and a club ruff. West must make sure that his partner is ruffing South's club winner, not his club loser. Winning the ♡Q at trick 2, West switches to the ♣K, South winning the ♣A. Now when West wins the ♡A he returns the ♣J; if South covers with his ♣Q East ruffs, and if not, West wins the trick and plays another club for East to ruff. In all, the defence will take a club trick, a club ruff, and two trump tricks. Leading the ♣K does not give away West's club trick — it simply establishes the ♣J or ♣10 as a winner instead.

HAND 17 • *What Rixi Said*

If declarer starts out by playing the ♠K , East wins and plays the ♡K followed by the ♣Q won in dummy. Say declarer ruffs a heart, crosses to hand on the ◇A, draws one round of spades with the ♠Q and then runs diamonds, planning to throw a club when East ruffs in with the master trump. East ruffs and returns a club anyway, and West's ♠7 is promoted to a winner for the setting trick. Nor does it help declarer to omit drawing the second trump after ruffing the heart. When East ruffs in and returns a club the ♠7 will still be established as a winner. If declarer does not ruff a heart but plays diamonds, discarding a club as East ruffs with the ♠J, East can simply return a trump and with no remaining entries to dummy South will have to lose a heart at the end for one down. If South overruffs the ♠J and ruffs a heart, discarding a club when East ruffs the next diamond, the trump promotion is still available for the defence for one down again.

Mrs. Markus found a different line. She led a small spade off dummy, winning the ♠Q, and then started to run diamonds. She writes "nothing could save East now for I was able to take discards on diamonds, whether she ruffed or not, and this restricted the defenders to two spades and a heart." On the hand as she played it, she was right. However, her statement does not quite hold true for the variation we have shown here.

Suppose East ruffs in on the third diamond, South throwing a small heart, and continues with the ♡K. Wriggle as she might, South will have to face same trump promotion. If she wins the heart, crosses to dummy on the ♣A, and plays another diamond discarding a club or heart, East ruffs in, cashes the remaining plain suit winner and then leads a club through.

It seems Rixi was right when she said that many hands which are made could have been defeated!

HAND 18 • *The Exception*

After declarer draws trumps and leads a spade towards the dummy, West might consider ducking. However, this does not work. If declarer puts in the ♠9 and then leads a club to the ♣10 and ♣Q, West will find himself endplayed in three suits. Playing the ♣A will establish a diamond discard in dummy on the ♣K, a spade will establish dummy's ♠J for a diamond discard in hand and a diamond will reduce the defenders' winners in that suit to two. In any case, South will have no more than three losers. Therefore, West must take the ♠Q.

Now to defeat the contract, West plays the ♣A and the ♣Q. While this may not be the standard way to play the suit West should realize that to defeat the contract East must have either the ♣K or ♣J. If East has the ♣K then it doesn't matter which club he returns but if East has the ♣J then he must protect this card (which is not subject to a ruffing finesse) by returning the ♣Q. Declarer cannot cope with this defence. He can discard a diamond from dummy on the ♣K and a diamond from hand on the ♠J but he still has two diamond losers and the defence prevails.

HAND 19 • *Mrs. Guggenheim*

This hand can be made and it only takes a very simple alteration in declarer's line; perhaps the legendary Mrs. Guggenheim might have made this hand. The trick is to throw a spade on the fourth club. Now when you cash the two top diamonds and lead the ◇ J, and East wins the ◇ Q you arrive at this position:

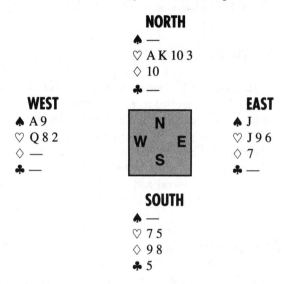

NORTH
♠ —
♡ A K 10 3
◇ 10
♣ —

WEST
♠ A 9
♡ Q 8 2
◇ —
♣ —

EAST
♠ J
♡ J 9 6
◇ 7
♣ —

SOUTH
♠ —
♡ 7 5
◇ 9 8
♣ 5

The only troublesome lead by East is the ♠J. But South ruffs, discarding the blocking ◇ 10 from dummy. Now he can cash the established diamonds in the closed hand before taking the last two tricks with the ace-king of hearts.

HAND 20 • *A Sure Bet*

This hand can be made. First declarer must take the safety play in clubs by playing a club to dummy's ♣J at trick 2. East must duck this since, otherwise, we now have twelve top tricks. Declarer now cashes the ♣K and dummy's clubs are set up — without a loser. Now declarer can afford to force an entry to dummy in diamonds by leading a small diamond to dummy's ◇ 10. Whether the defence wins this trick or not, dummy can be entered in diamonds and the clubs cashed to make the contract.

HAND 21 • *You Have to See This*

There is one more twist to this neat hand. Instead of ruffing the ♣Q, East pitches his last heart! Now South's diamond loser is gone, but he still can't make the hand: continuing clubs doesn't work (there are just too many hearts to get rid of), and whatever declarer tries, sooner or later West gets in with the ♠A, and gives this partner a heart ruff.

HAND 22 • *An Early Warning*

This hand *can* be made. After one round of trumps, when the ♡Q fell, declarer had an early warning. Declarer now abandons trumps and tries three rounds of clubs. When the clubs break 3-3, declarer can play the fourth club discarding a diamond from dummy. If East ruffs this club, declarer can enter dummy with the third heart to cash the top spades. If East discards, declarer can duck a diamond and win the trump return, and still has a trump in dummy to ruff his last diamond loser.

HAND 23 • *Cardinal Sin*

This hand *cannot* be made on best defence. Declarer's best chance to score ten tricks is to try to ruff two clubs in dummy. East switches to a trump at trick 2 but declarer will continue a club. If East wins this trick he will have no trumps to return and declarer will be able to score his ruffs. Say East returns a diamond. Declarer rises with the ◇K, ruffs a club and crosses to his hand with a heart ruff to ruff the last club. Finally he can get back to his hand ruffing a heart high and drawing the remaining trumps. But there is a way to defeat this hand. West must make the cardinal sin of ruffing his partner's club trick when declarer leads a club at trick three. Now the defence can lead a second trump and declarer will inevitably fall a trick short.

HAND 24 • *Helen Sobel*

Helen Sobel found a simple solution. At trick two she led the ◇Q! West won and could do no better than to lead a spade,

Helen winning. Now Helen cashed the ◇ A and drew three rounds of trumps ending in dummy. She took her spade pitch on the ◇ J and still had two trumps left in hand, so that she could give up two club tricks and set up the fourth club while staying in control of the hand.

HAND 25 • *Technical Play*

The contract is now 100%. All you have to do once the ♣Q holds is to lead the ♠10 and duck it. If East wins you now have two more entries to dummy to finesse clubs. If the spade holds (whoever has the ♠Q), you now revert back to clubs — simply conceding a trick to East. You have three spade tricks, a diamond, a heart and four clubs. No points for just guessing the ♠Q. The whole hand is:

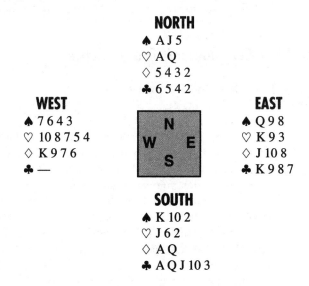

NORTH
♠ A J 5
♡ A Q
◇ 5 4 3 2
♣ 6 5 4 2

WEST
♠ 7 6 4 3
♡ 10 8 7 5 4
◇ K 9 7 6
♣ —

EAST
♠ Q 9 8
♡ K 9 3
◇ J 10 8
♣ K 9 8 7

SOUTH
♠ K 10 2
♡ J 6 2
◇ A Q
♣ A Q J 10 3

HAND 26 • *Thinking It Through*

This hand *can* be made. Declarer should anticipate this problem. After winning the ♠J and cashing the ◇ A, declarer should continue with the ♡Q, which East has to duck. Now declarer continues with a heart to the ♡10, and whether East ducks or wins, South has nine tricks.

HAND 27 • *No Respect*

This hand *can* be made, but South must pay the respect due to a king. South simply ducks the ♠K, losing an unnecessary spade trick. Now South can win whatever West returns (a club is best), cash the ♣A, cross on the ♠K and take the ruffing finesse in clubs. East covers and South can re-enter dummy with the ♠5 throwing two diamond losers and gaining two tricks for the one given up.

HAND 28 • *Jean Besse's Hand*

When Jean Besse was in with the ◇Q, he did not switch to the ♣K, he switched to the ♣J! West won the ♣A and continued a club to Besse's ♣K. Now Jean was on lead to lead a club through declarer's ♣86 to his partner's ♣97, defeating the contract.

HAND 29 • *Give Yourself Every Chance*

If the ♣Q is onside, singleton, two or three times, or even four times with a singleton ace on the left you can make four club tricks, and you won't need five heart tricks. The best play is to overtake the ♡Q with the ♡K and play a small club to the ♣10. If it loses to the ♣A on your left, you are home as long as the defense cannot take more than three diamond tricks. Regardless of the distribution you can re-enter dummy with a second heart and cannot be prevented from getting four club tricks, three heart tricks, one spade and one diamond. If East has the ♣A and ♣Q, you may still make it, if hearts are 3-3, or if he has only two or three clubs. (If East has four clubs to the AQ he will duck the ♣2 when you lead it from dummy and you will not be able to get more than three club tricks.) The full hand was :

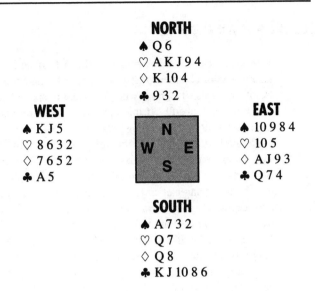

NORTH
♠ Q 6
♡ A K J 9 4
◇ K 10 4
♣ 9 3 2

WEST
♠ K J 5
♡ 8 6 3 2
◇ 7 6 5 2
♣ A 5

EAST
♠ 10 9 8 4
♡ 10 5
◇ A J 9 3
♣ Q 7 4

SOUTH
♠ A 7 3 2
♡ Q 7
◇ Q 8
♣ K J 10 8 6

HAND 30 • *Lucky Spots*

This hand *can* be defeated. East had the right idea by winning the ♠A and switching to a heart, but he must switch to the ♡10. If declarer takes the ♡A and starts diamonds, the defence switches back to spades when they win the first diamond, eventually taking two spades, two diamonds and a heart. If declarer ducks the heart to the ♡Q, East wins the first diamond and continues hearts. When West gets in on the second diamond, he can lead his remaining heart. East is sitting with the king-eight over dummy's jack-five. In all the defence takes five tricks: two hearts, two diamonds and the ♠A.

HAND 31 • *Step By Step*

This hand *can* be made. Declarer must take the hand step by step. First, declarer leads out the ♠Q before drawing trumps. West must duck or else he sets up two spade winners in the North hand. Now declarer abandons spades and ducks a diamond. After winning the return, declarer draws exactly two rounds of trumps and then ruffs the fourth diamond is dummy. East, who has the long trump, must follow to this trick. In all declarer loses a diamond and two clubs.

HAND 32 • *It All Depends*

If you can count on West to win the ♣K if he has it, you can improve your chances greatly, and, in fact, make the hand on this lie of the cards. Declarer wins the opening spade lead in dummy and finesses the ♣Q. If this holds, then declarer can safety play the heart suit while creating an entry back to dummy. Declarer plays the ♡A and ♡K and then plays the ♡J, throwing away the ♠A from hand. Now when East wins the ♡Q, he must give South the dummy or abandon the spade suit completely; anything else helps declarer even more. If East returns a spade, declarer can repeat the club finesse for nine tricks after running hearts. If the defense plays diamonds, declarer can cash his diamond winners and exit with a small club. The defence will be forced to lead a black suit. Note that, if the club finesse had lost, declarer could still fall back on playing for a 'perfect' position in the heart suit (♡Qxx onside).

HAND 33 • *Impress the Kibitzers*

This hand can be made. The simple play is the right play on this hand. Ruff the opening spade lead and try to cash the top three diamonds. This wins when diamonds are 3-3, but it also wins when the diamonds are no worse than 5-1 and the long club hand has the short diamonds, as on this hand. East ruffs in on the second diamond and continues a heart. Declarer now draws the trumps ending in dummy. He then cashes the ♠A throwing the third and blocking diamond from the South hand and can now discard the two heart losers on the long diamonds. If East doesn't ruff in on the second diamond, South plays a third diamond. Even if East discards on this, South can discard two hearts anyway, one on the ♠A and then a second on the ◇J which East can now ruff if he wants.

HAND 34 • *Raising the Dead*

After winning the ◇A and drawing three rounds of trumps, declarer cashes the ◇K hoping for the best, but West shows out. At this stage, you have only one chance. You will need West to hold both the ♠J and the ♣A. Cashing the ♠A, you enter dummy with the ♠10 and lead the ♣K, throwing the ♠K from your hand. Now West is endplayed and must play a spade or club allowing you to enter dummy. You can throw one diamond loser on the ♠Q and the other on the ♣Q. This is the whole hand:

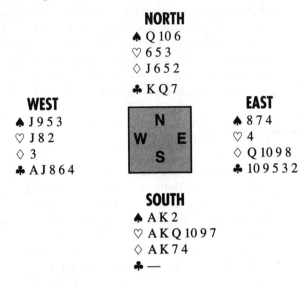

NORTH
♠ Q 10 6
♡ 6 5 3
◇ J 6 5 2
♣ K Q 7

WEST
♠ J 9 5 3
♡ J 8 2
◇ 3
♣ A J 8 6 4

EAST
♠ 8 7 4
♡ 4
◇ Q 10 9 8
♣ 10 9 5 3 2

SOUTH
♠ A K 2
♡ A K Q 10 9 7
◇ A K 7 4
♣ —

HAND 35 • *A Rare Ending*

It is far more likely that East has the ♣A only, as opposed to specifically the ♣AQ without the ♣10. The key is to lose the first club trick to East. Declarer simply leads the ♣K from his hand, after cashing three diamonds. East can get out a club or cash the ♠A, but either way declarer is in control and has time to establish his club trick.

HAND 36 • *Play It Safe*

This hand *cannot* be made. It is true that after three rounds of diamonds, East discarding a heart, South can make the hand by endplaying East. Declarer cashes the ♠A and two rounds of hearts and leads a spade. East must give declarer a ruff-sluff or return a club, either way allowing declarer to escape without a club loser. But East can beat the hand by ruffing in on the third round of diamonds with the ♠K. A discard from the South hand is not helpful and now there is no endplay. East can safely exit with a trump or a heart and South will eventually have a club loser.

HAND 37 • *There Is a Way*

This hand *cannot* be made on best defence. If West switches to ♣A and ♣Q then declarer can make the hand by ruffing his remaining club loser with dummy's ♠6. The way to defeat the hand is to switch to the ♣Q! This takes out dummy's club entry but West retains control of the club suit. Whether declarer plays a diamond or a club at trick three, the defence can win and return a trump leaving South with an inevitable club loser.

HAND 38 • *Last Chance*

This contract *cannot* be made on best defence. Winning the ♣K, West must shift to the ♠Q, seizing the defence's last chance to remove dummy's entry! East ducks this spade and now declarer has no entry to dummy to cash the clubs when they are established. Declarer still has the faint hope of endplaying East. Winning the second club, West must continue spades and if declarer plays low from dummy, East will duck again. Now declarer can cash his winners but will only have eight tricks: two spades, three hearts, and three diamonds.

HAND 39 • *A Meagre Clue*

If East has the ◇A, he can be endplayed. Drawing the last trump, ending in dummy, declarer cashes the ♠K and leads a small diamond from dummy to the ◇Q. If West is able to win this with the ◇A, declarer has to hope that West also holds the ♣K. But if the ◇Q holds, then declarer leads a diamond towards dummy's ◇K and plays low on whatever card West plays. Of course this works in the unlikely case that East has the doubleton ◇A. But in all other cases, West wins the trick and does best to switch to the ♣J which declarer ducks in dummy and wins with the ♣A. Now declarer continues with a diamond to the king which East must win, whereupon he is endplayed. The whole hand is:

NORTH
♠ K 2
♡ A Q 8 4 3
♢ K 8 3
♣ Q 7 5

WEST
♠ J 10 9 7
♡ J 6 5
♢ 10 9 6
♣ J 10 3

```
      N
   W     E
      S
```

EAST
♠ Q 6 5 4 3
♡ —
♢ A J 7 2
♣ K 9 4 2

SOUTH
♠ A 8
♡ K 10 9 7 2
♢ Q 5 4
♣ A 8 6

HAND 40 • *A Lucky Mistake*

When this hand was played, declarer made a very lucky mistake. After ruffing a club at trick 4, he led the ♢ Q from his hand. This play actually gives declarer a lot of extra chances. West must win and is endplayed — if he returns a spade, South can duck in dummy and pick up the spade suit for no losers and if he returns a diamond, South has an extra diamond trick, and can ruff his spade loser in dummy. Even if West had more clubs, the contract is cold — if West returns a club declarer can now establish the club suit, no matter how it splits, and has ample entries to get to dummy to cash the club winners.

HAND 41 • *Handling Charges*

This hand *can* be made. After winning the ♢ A, East shifts to a club won by South's ♣ A. Declarer now cashes the ♢ K shedding a club. The ♡ 8 is now led from the South hand. West must not win the ♡ A since otherwise declarer is in control after forcing out the ♠ A, and West must cover ♡ 8 with the ♡ 10 to try to establish the heart blockage seen before. Now South plays the ♠ K, ducked by East. At this point, the simplest line is for declarer to play another spade. East wins, and we arrive at this position:

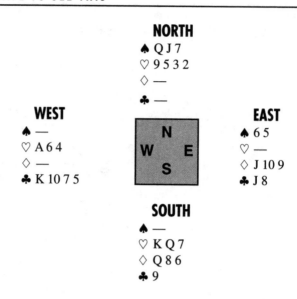

NORTH
♠ Q J 7
♡ 9 5 3 2
◇ —
♣ —

WEST
♠ —
♡ A 6 4
◇ —
♣ K 10 7 5

EAST
♠ 6 5
♡ —
◇ J 10 9
♣ J 8

SOUTH
♠ —
♡ K Q 7
◇ Q 8 6
♣ 9

Whatever West returns declarer can crossruff the hand. Let us say that West returns a spade. North ruffs, and it does no good for East to overruff since dummy would be high after declarer drew East's last two trumps. Now declarer leads the ◇Q. If East discards, South discards and declarer can now cross-ruff the hand. If East ruffs, then South overruffs and continues the cross-ruff. It doesn't help East to overruff later and return his last trump since dummy will win and play the high spades.

The play requires this precise sequence, or a minor variation of it, but the hand is cold!

HAND 42 • *The Crane Hand*

This hand *should not* be made, despite the fine play at trick two in the heart suit by declarer. The defence does have a counter: they must prevent South from getting to dummy. To do that East must hold off on the ♡K. South's best play now is to cash all his black suit winners. The defence must not ruff any of these tricks and must keep all their spades! Now declarer is forced to lead a heart won by East. East exits a spade and when West gains the lead on the ♡A, he has a spade left to exit, endplaying declarer who must now lead a diamond from the KJ.

HAND 43 • *At the World Championships*

The commentators were right, this hand *cannot* be made, but only if the defence finds an incredible play that was not found at the table. Declarer's only chance is to establish the diamond suit. Declarer ruffs the opening lead and plays diamonds. East wins and continues clubs, South ruffing. South continues with another diamond. If West wins the ◇K and continues clubs, declarer ruffs, cashes the ♡A and crosses on the ♠K and plays diamonds. At this stage the hand is cold. East must ruff a diamond and South overruffs, shortening East's trumps to two. Now declarer plays a spade to dummy and runs diamonds. Whether East ruffs the spade or not, declarer is in control.

But what if West ducks the second diamond? A crossruff won't work: declarer now has two non-trump tricks but can only make seven trump tricks because East can overruff dummy's ♡5. If declarer continues with a diamond, East can throw his spade as West wins the diamond. West continues a club and this is the position with declarer needing all the tricks but one:

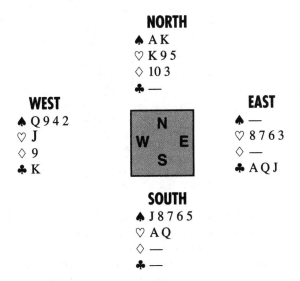

NORTH
♠ A K
♡ K 9 5
◇ 10 3
♣ —

WEST
♠ Q 9 4 2
♡ J
◇ 9
♣ K

EAST
♠ —
♡ 8 7 6 3
◇ —
♣ A Q J

SOUTH
♠ J 8 7 6 5
♡ A Q
◇ —
♣ —

If declarer leads a spade to the ace as before, East ruffs in and plays a fourth club. If South ruffs in hand, he cannot get to dummy without setting up a trump trick for East so he must ruff in dummy. He now tries a diamond which gets ruffed and overruffed but he is once again stuck in his hand since crossing on a trump will leave East in control. Other lines involving cashing the ♠A before leading the diamond will also not work if West continues clubs, since they arrive at a similar position.

HAND 44 • *Perfection?*

This hand *can* still be made, even with perfect defence. At the table, West returned a diamond. Declarer won the ◊A correctly (if he ducks, East wins, gives West a spade ruff and the defence cashes the ♣A). Next came the ♡Q and then a club from dummy. East correctly ducked (since if he rises, he will be forced to get out a club, the ♣K winning and East once again subject to a squeeze). Declarer won the ♣K, arriving at this end position:

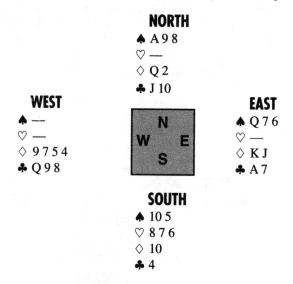

NORTH
♠ A 9 8
♡ —
◊ Q 2
♣ J 10

WEST
♠ —
♡ —
◊ 9 7 5 4
♣ Q 9 8

EAST
♠ Q 7 6
♡ —
◊ K J
♣ A 7

SOUTH
♠ 10 5
♡ 8 7 6
◊ 10
♣ 4

If declarer plays a club now, West will win and play a diamond. East will win the ◊J and continue the ◊K breaking up the squeeze. Declarer must instead run hearts in the diagrammed position; without rectifying the count, the squeeze does not operate but East's last four cards must include two spades. Whether he keeps two diamonds, or a diamond and the ♣A, a diamond and a small club, he will eventually be endplayed in spades. Sometimes even perfect defence will be defeated by perfect play.

HAND 45 • *A Good Idea*

This hand *can* be made. South had a good idea in discarding a club on the ♠A instead of a diamond. But the first step in making this hand is to set up a second spade winner. Winning the opening spade lead, declarer should continue another spade discarding a second club. West will win and return a trump or a spade. South wins the ♡A and discards his third club on the ♠10. The next step is to set up the thirteenth club as declarer's twelfth trick. Cashing the ♣A, South crosses to dummy on trumps. Being careful to handle the trump spot cards carefully to ensure three entries, he first ruffs two clubs and then returns to dummy a third time to cash the established club for his slam-going trick.

HAND 46 • *A Master At Play*

This hand *can always* be made. Belladonna made the hand on a trump squeeze. Belladonna played three rounds of trumps and noted East's two diamond discards. Deducing that East was 1-4-5-3 and deciding to place him with the ♣Q, he played a fourth round of trumps and threw all the clubs from dummy. This was the ending when South had led a spade and thrown a club from dummy. East is to play and has no good discard:

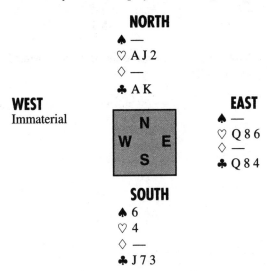

```
                    NORTH
                    ♠ —
                    ♡ A J 2
                    ◇ —
                    ♣ A K
    WEST                              EAST
    Immaterial         N             ♠ —
                    W     E          ♡ Q 8 6
                       S             ◇ —
                                     ♣ Q 8 4
                    SOUTH
                    ♠ 6
                    ♡ 4
                    ◇ —
                    ♣ J 7 3
```

If East throws a club, South can cash the ♣AK and ruff a heart to hand scoring the ♣J. If East discards a heart South can set the suit up with one ruff and return to dummy with a club to enjoy dummy's last heart.

Suppose Jacoby switches to the ♡10 at trick 2 before cashing the second diamond. The ♡10 is covered by the ♡J, and the ♡K wins. If the defence cashes a second diamond before playing a second heart the same trump squeeze operates. If the defence continues hearts and does not cash the second diamond, declarer ruffs a heart and runs all the trumps arriving at this ending:

NORTH
♠ —
♡ 7
♢ —
♣ A K 10

WEST
Immaterial

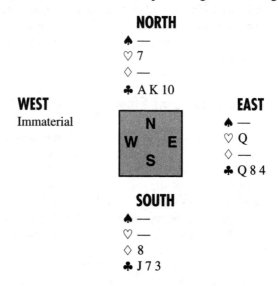

EAST
♠ —
♡ Q
♢ —
♣ Q 8 4

SOUTH
♠ —
♡ —
♢ 8
♣ J 7 3

Now a club is played to the ♣A and a heart from dummy end-plays Wolff.

HAND 47 • *A Strange Endplay*

This hand *can* be made; declarer was on the right track. Declarer draws all three trumps and continues with five rounds of diamonds, throwing two spades and a club from dummy and arriving at this ending:

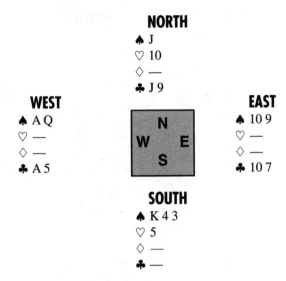

NORTH
♠ J
♡ 10
◇ —
♣ J 9

WEST
♠ A Q
♡ —
◇ —
♣ A 5

EAST
♠ 10 9
♡ —
◇ —
♣ 10 7

SOUTH
♠ K 4 3
♡ 5
◇ —
♣ —

South now leads a small spade, West winning with the ♠Q. This is the one and only trick for the defence. It works equally well if West holds onto ♠A Q 8 and ♣A. The key to the hand is to keep exactly one spade, the ♠J, in dummy. This allows declarer to endplay West who must win this spade trick.

HAND 48 • *Smothered*

This hand *cannot* be made. If declarer believes that the ♠J is a true card, he can play for a smother play. He ruffs a heart, cashes three round of diamonds, crosses to dummy on the ♣A and ruffs a heart, cashes the ♣K and exits a club in this ending:

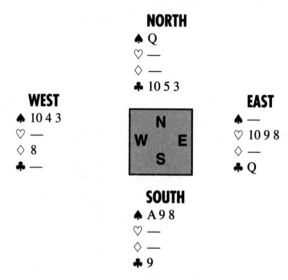

NORTH
♠ Q
♡ —
♢ —
♣ 10 5 3

WEST
♠ 10 4 3
♡ —
♢ 8
♣ —

EAST
♠ —
♡ 10 9 8
♢ —
♣ Q

SOUTH
♠ A 9 8
♡ —
♢ —
♣ 9

If East wins the club trick, West throwing a diamond, then South will make the hand. East will have to lead a heart, South will ruff with the ♠9, and whether West overruffs or not South will make the rest of the tricks. But if West ruffs his partner's club trick he can defeat the hand. He must return a trump. Declarer has to win the ♠Q and come off dummy with a club — promoting West's ♠10!

HAND 49 • *The Moysian Fit*

This hand *should not* be made. West must duck the ♣K.
Declarer will continue with the ♣Q and ♣J and West continues
to duck, East winning the third round with a ruff, leading to this
7-card ending:

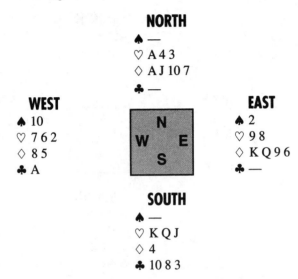

NORTH
♠ —
♡ A 4 3
◇ A J 10 7
♣ —

WEST
♠ 10
♡ 7 6 2
◇ 8 5
♣ A

EAST
♠ 2
♡ 9 8
◇ K Q 9 6
♣ —

SOUTH
♠ —
♡ K Q J
◇ 4
♣ 10 8 3

East must now continue a spade, giving declarer a ruff-sluff and
continuing the pressure on declarer's trump suit. South ruffs in
dummy and can return once on a trump to his hand to ruff out the
♣A with the ♡A, but cannot get back to his hand without forcing himself in diamonds. He cannot now draw trumps and enjoy
his long club since West will have the long trump.

HAND 50 • *At the Blue Ribbon*

This hand *can* be made on a "clash squeeze". The key is to run diamonds before playing the top spades. After drawing trumps and playing two rounds of clubs, declarer returns to his hand by ruffing the third club, reaching this position:

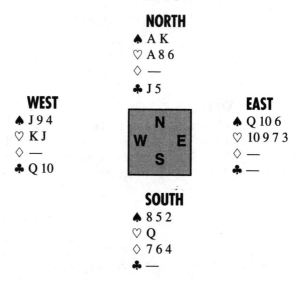

NORTH
♠ A K
♡ A 8 6
◇ —
♣ J 5

WEST
♠ J 9 4
♡ K J
◇ —
♣ Q 10

EAST
♠ Q 10 6
♡ 10 9 7 3
◇ —
♣ —

SOUTH
♠ 8 5 2
♡ Q
◇ 7 6 4
♣ —

On the next diamond, West cannot afford to throw a club or declarer can ruff out the ♣Q. If he throws a spade, declarer will have a double squeeze with hearts as the central suit by cashing the top two spades, ruffing a club and playing off the trumps; therefore he must throw his penultimate heart and dummy also throws a heart. But on the next diamond West is done. He still cannot throw a black card for the same reasons and if he throws the 'useless' ♡K, South's ♡Q is set up for the thirteenth trick. Note that since West has the club guard this squeeze will work any time that West has the ♡K.

HAND 51 • *A Classic Deal*

Declarer can play West for a doubleton honour in clubs by cashing the ♣A and then ducking a club to West's ♣Q. West cannot unblock the ♣Q under the ace for declarer can then lead up to the ♣J, losing only one club trick. West is thus endplayed with the ♣Q, forced to give declarer a ruff-sluff. Declarer discards a club from dummy and now can ruff his two losing clubs with dummy's remaining trumps.

However, there is more to this story. West is marked with a 6-4 hand so at trick one East knows that in order to defeat the contract the defence must take either two club tricks or a club and a trump. Taking two club tricks is only possible if West has the ♣Q. But if West has the ♣Qx, as in the actual hand, he can, as we have seen, be subjected to the endplay which *The Bridge World* calls a "Classic A-J Elimination". Therefore East must overtake the ♡K with the ♡A and switch to the ♣10 at trick 2, covered by the ♣J, ♣Q and ♣A. Declarer can draw trumps and eliminate diamonds as before but now when he plays a heart, West can win and lead a club through dummy's ♣97: East must score two tricks with the ♣K8. And if, at trick 2, South ducks the ♣10 in hand, winning the ♣A in dummy, then when West eventually gets in with the ♣Q he can cash the ♡K and safely exit with his third high heart: East must eventually score a second club trick.

You may wonder why East-West are defending on these cards. We don't know, but let's allow them to make up for their bidding misjudgement by defending superbly!

HAND 52 • *A Sweet Ending*

This hand *can always* be made. After winning the ♡A, East switched to A♠ and another spade. Declarer played a diamond, West winning the ♢10 and continuing a heart to declarer's king. Now declarer plays off all the trumps but one to arrive at this very sweet ending:

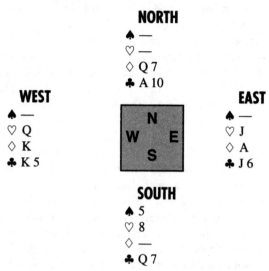

NORTH
♠ —
♡ —
♢ Q 7
♣ A 10

WEST
♠ —
♡ Q
♢ K
♣ K 5

EAST
♠ —
♡ J
♢ A
♣ J 6

SOUTH
♠ 5
♡ 8
♢ —
♣ Q 7

On the last spade North discards a diamond, and the defence is in trouble. Both defenders must keep two clubs and therefore each of them must guard a different red suit. Declarer now simply plays a heart, and endplays the defender who has the last heart. That defender must lead a club and whether it is West or East, declarer can make it by guessing the ending. At the table East chose instead to discard a club on the last spade. Declarer made the hand by leading the ♣Q, smothering the ♣J, and setting up the ♣10.

What if East ducks the opening heart trick to declarer? Now South can duck a diamond and, since he still has his trump entry to dummy, he will be able to ruff a second diamond setting up the simple diamond/club squeeze on West. The defence will take either two hearts and a spade or two spades and a heart to go along with their diamond trick.